THE COMING
MUSLIM
WORLD DOMINATION

by JAYSON X. GROSSMANN

The loss of Western Civilization
is coming due to the lack of a long-term
United States strategy

Revised and updated from
First private Edition 2008

Copyright 2009 by Jason X. Grossmann

ISBN: 978-0-9824931-2-0

Published by:

FL Publishers
North Fort Myers, FL 33903
(239) 652-0135

www.FLPublishers.com

Printed in the United States of America
18 17 16 15 14 13 12 11 10 09   2 3 4 5 6

DEDICATION

Susan McDougal
The woman who could not be made to talk.

Fabrizio Quattrocchi
The man who said: "Now I will show you
how an Italian dies."

Arayel, my co-worker

TABLE OF CONTENTS

INTRODUCTION

None lived forever

Could the U.S. be at the zenith of its power after more than two centuries of uninterrupted progress and increasing political power? Is there some kind of rule or law governing the collapse of great nations?

Is there an inevitable cycle of birth, growth and decay just like we see in plants, humans, animals and even in solar systems?

Were there common factors in the decline of the Roman Empire as well as the Spanish, Dutch and British colonial-maritime powers? And, why did the Nazi dictatorship last only a little more than a decade, while oppressive Russian Communism existed more than 70 years? Or, should these widely divergent phenomena be compared to organisms that are being attacked by some kind of deadly virus, the one dying more quickly than the other?

One thing is obvious: none lived forever. However, the Roman Empire, stretching from Europe far into Asia and, secondly, Great Britain with its vast overseas possessions had more staying power than the rest.

One obviously common factor in the decline and fall of nations appears to be a lack of will or capability to budget enough funds for the military, whether in defense or offense, or both.

Rome ran out of money at the beginning of the Dark Ages, eighteenth-century Holland was outspent by the British in maritime expansion, Germany lost its shirt waging a costly, unwise two-front war, the Soviets went broke trying to match Reagan's enormous "Star War" project, while Great Britain's decline began in 1939 when its military defenses were down. As soon as the U.S. got involved in 1941, its huge armies and supplies of weaponry became the decisive factor in the war against Germany. Then, after defeating Japan, the U.S. supported worldwide abolition of colonialism, quickly becoming a superpower.

So how long does the U.S. get to hold on to its present status at the top? Are the small-scale struggles of the Western nations in Afghanistan and Iraq a prelude to more wars against Islamist expansion that will eventually sap their economies? Would a failure in Iraq encourage extremist growth? Is it the policy of Al Qaida to keep the West bogged down in these wars that can't be won and over a period of time, bleed the U.S. into bankruptcy? Why is the present confrontation with militant Islam in the Middle East more in the nature of a "soft" war with low casualties as compared with the "hard", all-out wars of the 1940s? Are the Islamists just as dangerous as the Nazis or the Communists were or do they invade the world more like an inoperable cancer?

You can be sure Al Qaida is aware of the limits of the U.S. war-machine, which is in knee-jerk low gear because of America's ever growing hunger for Middle East oil and the necessity to stay on friendly terms with the Muslim world.

If the U.S. cannot satisfactorily deal with the above questions, it will soon become difficult to keep its oily dance on the Middle East tightrope balanced. All its present military strategies are too short-term as well; it lacks a longer view stretching into the next hundred years. It is at a crossroads.

The purpose of this book is to advance arguments for the setting of several Machiavellian traps that will paralyze future Muslim expansionism. The Muslim jihad is craftily exploiting western softness, using ambushes, women, mosques and suicides vests as "holy weapons" instead of engaging the enemy on large open fronts. This strategy can be undone by some equally western dirty deeds done dirt-cheap that will be explained below.

Is the U.S. too timid to meet dirt with dirt? The author predicts that the West, including the U.S., will dilly-dally due to internal division until catastrophe is at its doorstep.

That catastrophe, the Third World War, will probably occur within the next twenty-five years, at a cost of lives far exceeding casualties of the 1940s. The West will probably win that most horrible of all horrible wars. But despite that win, the author, using indisputable facts and calculations, will show that within a hundred years the Islamic domination of the entire world, along with the destruction of much of the West's hard-won culture, will have become a reality.

The author predicts that the U.S. will not be able to prevent World War III, because it will continue its naïve, soft methods. An old Indian friend of mine once said: "Soft medicine men make stinking wounds."

Unless, unless, the U.S. gets tougher and wilier than its enemy from now on—unless the U.S. starts performing the necessary strategic surgery in the Middle East now, the end result will be its inevitable doom sometime between the years 2100 and 2125.

1.   THE BIG BANG

America's weak response

When, what is now infamously known as 9/11, came smashing into world history, it signaled one Osama Bin Laden's virtual challenge to America's status of superpower. At the same time it raised him to superhero in the entire Muslim world. Let us make no mistake—his popularity and influence amongst the Muslims is huge, equaling or surpassing that of individual Muslim political leaders by far. He can declare Jihad, Holy War, on behalf of the entire Muslim world.

How? He heads Al Qaida, a growing movement that, in accordance with the Holy Quran, intends to establish Islam as the only religion on earth. All practicing Muslims, even those—believe it or not—that live in the United States, subscribe to that idea. They have to. He sent thousands of troops to Kosovo to fight the Serbs, he has his hand in the Sudan crisis, in the Iraq dilemma, in the Gaza revolt and other places. In a later chapter we will see the texts in which the Prophet Mohammed says that all "infidels" must eventually submit to Islam under Sharia law.

The damage caused by the 9/11 suicide hijackers of the planes was immense, catastrophic, out of all proportion to the fraction it took Al Qaida to organize and execute the attack. And while the whole world held its breath, waiting for an immediate response, America did nothing. Unlike the quick internment of the Japanese-Americans after Pearl Harbor, to do something like that to the 4 or 5 million Muslims in the country was unthinkable under the changed rules adopted by the United Nations. So, by reverse logic, in order to show no racial or religious bias, the American public

9

as a whole was soon forced to undergo heavy-handed scrutiny via the Homeland Security and Patriot Acts at airports, in telecommunications and through increased police powers of surveillance and detainment. In other words, all Americans are being punished for something nineteen enemy Muslims did. Bin Laden must have grinned at this double victory. But now comes the ID card like in Nazi Germany. What will be next? A police state? Is the A.C.L.U. asleep?

So who was the U.S. to hit first? Bin Laden? I have talked to many people who said that if the U.S. had forthwith made a more explicit declaration of war and had then, without asking permission from the U.N. or any country involved, followed up with a medium-sized nuclear weapon, directed at a specific target in the sparsely populated, mountainous Tora Bora region where Bin Laden was known to be headquartered, it would have been game over for Al Qaida for a long time. I think that if at the same time the U.S. had agreed to let Israel smash certain targets in the Gaza strip with a continuous, day long artillery barrage, its problems with the Palestinians would have been solved for a long, long time as well.

This kind of response would also have served as a sample of what would happen in any future Islamist sneak terrorist attack. Any further Muslim carnage would not just be answered in like measure, but tenfold. If ten times as many Muslims had died for the victims in the U.S., it would have fallen into that category. Few American soldiers' lives would subsequently have been lost in the war on terrorism. The oil would have kept on flowing and the staggering financial outlays for fighting terrorism would have been avoided.

No doubt, there would have been denunciations from several countries, but it would have been a done thing, not to be repeated in the foreseeable future. Even Russia and China would have understood that the American eagle, riled to the limit by the Muslim hornets, had the right to strike back hard, instantly, and with all its might and fury. Something to consider, if and when bin Laden sticks to his promise to once again strike a deadly blow at the heart of "infidel" America.

But the opportunity passed, maybe forever, and the result is a somewhat diminished level of America's status as the world's superpower. Deep down, the U.S. is afraid of "insulting Islam".

In the last year of the Clinton administration the U.S. made the unforgivable blunder of not killing bin Laden and his coterie when a plane had him in its crosshairs. Permission by Clinton was required, but he somehow "absented" himself and the archenemy of America disappeared.

During Bush's presidency—a similar gaffe: When U.S. aircraft were systematically dropping their ultra-heavy deeply penetrating bombs in the Tora Bora mountains in Afghanistan where bin Laden was hiding, the action was abruptly stopped when local tribesmen started howling about "civilian" deaths. Did some of the tunnels near bin Laden collapse? No doubt, the protesters were proxies for Al Qaida. Score another two points for the man.

The U.S. is too sensitive to Muslim complaints. The louder they scream, the harder they should be hit.

It seems that Israel is finally learning this lesson: hit Hamas so hard that they begin to respect the weapons of the "infidel" Jews. There is a relatively cheap trick, by which Israel can forever end the rain of Hamas rockets, but it cannot be told here; it is safely filed with my lawyer.

Remember when Israel threatened total war on Jordan unless it stopped the Palestinians from attacking across the border? Well, former King Hussein beat them so ruthlessly in the 1970 "Black September" battle that the border between Jordan and Israel has been quiet ever since.

If small Jordan could do it, why cannot superpower America do the same thing in Iraq? The reason is that the U.S. has not yet found a strategy to counter Al Qaida's dirty tricks. That is the weak underbelly of the U.S. and bin Laden is well aware of it. So are the leaders of any given Muslim country who watch and smirk as they see tens of thousands of American troops butting their heads against small bands of inspired fanatics? Is bin Laden working to keep it that way?

The U.S. was so scared of hurting its fragile ties with the Middle East that it had to sit on its haunches for a year and a half before it could make an attack on a "safe" target— Iraq. Regardless of the casus belli, the so-called "Weapons of Mass Destruction flop", it was safe to attack Saddam Hussein because he was almost universally disliked and few Muslim regimes had any serious misgivings about the destruction of the cruel tyrant's power. The most graphic proof that it was Saddam the U.S. was after and not the WMDs was the theatrical hauling down of his massive statues. Cynics have it that the deep underlying motive of the Iraq adventure was continued future access to the country's vast oil reserves.

But, looking at it with a longer view, the author is of the opinion that the U.S. occupation of Iraq was also a tremendous masterstroke, because it is like a dagger, thrust into the heart of fundamentalist Islam, only the U.S. does not yet know how to twist it.

This "twist" as developed below, is the indispensable link in the main long-range strategies that can be used to turn the tide in Iraq and elsewhere in favor of the West. Not only do the short-term dirty tricks fit in, they connect with a broader plan for the future designed to take the wind out of the sails of all Muslim insurgencies forever, turning them against themselves. Instead, bin Laden is turning the U.S. war into a quagmire.

The author tried to interest two high-ranking politicians in these ideas, but was rebuffed by the following "sermon" that can be a lesson for everyone who intends to sell a government representative a novel idea. It was quickly pointed out to him that no single person in a Western government, not even a President or a Prime Minister, could change any policy in response to a well-meant, non-elected individual's suggestion. Decisions on foreign policy, including Iraq and Afghanistan, are not made by the President alone, but on the basis of existing policies previously adopted and, secondly, through the input of the Cabinet and scores of highly knowledgeable advisers and experts. No outsider, not even a past President, has a sliver of a chance to influence government policy. He or she would have to publish a book, get a large following or form a lobby group

So the purpose of this book is not to convince the government of anything, but to warn the public that America's coming decline will be due to the long-term consequences of short-term strategy. Short-term decisions as examined in this book will often lead to immense negative effects for future generations

In view of this, serious criticism of government policy is warranted. Thousands of people and organizations do it. The author will show how easily difficult goals such as a victory in Iraq, the prevention of a Third World War and the defeat of all Islamist insurgencies can be reached and how inelegantly the U.S. will do the exact opposite. Why? Because "that's how we have always done it and won", whether it was the War of Independence, the Spanish War, the two World Wars, the Korean War (half), the Vietnam

War (not) and now the War in the Middle East (when?). Mere force does not always bring victory. Moreover, war against Jihad proves to be unlike any other confrontation the U.S. has ever been involved in.

Stay the course or change it?

The U.S. is almost like a heavily laden train on an immovable track, heading for a washed out bridge. It cannot move left or right, but must "stay the course" to its destination. The question becomes: can it not turn into a "ship of state" again that can alter course, ninety degrees if necessary, when danger lurks?

Should we not heed Machiavelli's still valid warning that a conquered people will eventually oust an invading foreign army? He also pointed out that mercenary troops (in this case, Muslim allies) are often unreliable and can turn against their masters. And yes, the weapons America supplied to Afghanistan in its war against the Soviets as well as those with which it armed Saddam Hussein against Iran were soon turned against the U.S. like clockwork. Some of the equipment the U.S. entrusted to the Iraqis was sold for good cash to fellow Iraqis fighting the American soldiers. It is not safe to travel in the country, unless one joins a heavily armed convoy. Some of the Iraqi soldiers trained by the U.S. are Sunni infiltrators. Iraq has a huge black market in American-supplied food and other aid.

Also, a secular, western-type democracy in any Muslim country is almost unthinkable, because politics and war are regulated by the Quran and therefore under the jurisdiction of the clerics. It is well known that recently in Iran the candidates had to be approved by the clergy, eliminating the moderating influence of many secularly inclined Iranian politicians. By the same token we see that in Turkey, where since 1918 the army has been in charge of guarding the secular status of the government, more and more fundamentalists approved by the mullahs have been entering the government in several elections.

Amongst the few "precious" Muslim friends of the U.S. in the Middle East, those that stand out are Saudi Arabia, Egypt, Jordan and Turkey, but none of them are democracies with the freedoms, religious tolerance, broad education and human rights characterizing western democracies. In each of these four nations the regimes are well entrenched, but at the same time balanced with the clergy in a way that is unique for each country.

Al Sistani, the Ayatollah of predominantly Shia Iraq, has seen his stalwarts elected to the government. It is obvious that he partly controls al-Maliki and is playing the U.S. out against the remaining Sunnis until the latter are eliminated from politics in Iraq. Realistically speaking, it is totally disingenuous to try and reconcile Sunnis and Shias considering how much the latter suffered under the murderous rule of Saddam. They are sworn enemies; The U.S. asking for reconciliation is like Al Maliki asking the U.S. to cuddle with Al Qaida. It is ridiculous.

This is one of the major areas where the U.S. should change course. Killing Sunnis one day and Shias the next is as ludicrous as it is counterproductive. It creates nothing but hatred, both within Iraq and between Iraq and the U.S. We will come back to this matter later

The U.S. is also pursuing a fruitless endeavor for peace between the Palestinians and Israel. The whole idea is a farce. When Arafat was caught lying to the U.S. President re the smuggling of arms into Palestine, the U.S. changed its course with regard to Israel and quickly became more supportive. That those smuggled weapons came from Saudi Arabia, a country with which the U.S. must stay on friendly terms but which had been financing the Palestinian intifada for many years, highlights the perverse triangulation in which Israel can never hope to win and the Palestinians can never lose. The U.S. is undeniably in a bind and Israel in a perennial vise. There can never ever be peace between Israel and the Palestinians because the fight is not just against the Palestinians but against the entire Muslim world. Israel is the only country in the world that has taken over and annexed erstwhile Muslim territory and that, in the eyes of any Muslim believer—again, we must include those in the U.S.—is unpardonable sacrilege.

Here again, the U.S. must change its course. It should admit the illogic of peace between Israel and the Muslim world, based as it is on a fatal misunderstanding of the unchangeable, religious root cause of the conflict; it should lift its heavy diplomatic hand off Israel and let the country—without losing vital contact—pursue its own course in the destruction of the Palestinians, if and when a future violent attack on its cities calls for that. Let us never forget that Abbas is the heir of Arafat; both were united by the Muslim principle of never giving up Muslim land. Israel should make no deal with Abbas except one based on the status quo, More on the fortunes (or misfortunes) of Israel over the next hundred years in a later chapter.

What do the Muslim fundamentalists want?

All Muslims, whether fundamentalist or moderate, want the same thing: the eventual supremacy of Islam as the world's only religion.

16

A moderate is a person in favor of an idea or belief but does not cause a hubbub about it; the fundamentalist will fight for or otherwise actively promote an original dogma. Both believe in Allah's precepts regarding the infidels.

The Islamic fundamentalist, called Islamist in short, believes in using violence against any "infidel" who resists, condemns, fights or otherwise denies Islam. The Quran teaches him to kill all "unbelievers" who oppose the spread of Islam. For example, Pakistan wants all of Kashmir and it demands that India gently submit. Note that in this case it was an entire nation, fundamentalist Pakistan that fought for possession of that additional territory and got part of it. Islamist groups in India are quite active, causing periodic mayhem and murder. Islamic war for Allah (jihad) is always waged without mercy and generally with nauseating sadism.

The Prophet himself gave an example of how to deal with those who opposed him, when he massacred the Jewish tribe of Banu Quraiza, who had resisted him in the Battle of the Trench at Medina in the year 687. After their defeat, ditches were dug in the marketplace overnight. More than 700 Jewish men, shackled, in groups of half a dozen, were made to sit on the edges, and then beheaded and their bodies pitched into their graves. To top off his victory that night, Mohammed took one of the most beautiful Jewish women (whose husband, grown sons and hired men had just been slaughtered) to bed with him. As was the custom, the other women and children were sold into slavery—houses, cattle and money were taken as loot and divided. There was not a more efficient way to totally Islamize an entire Jewish hostile tribe. It was the standard method in all Muslim battles in the Islamic conquest of the Middle East. That is how Islam grew so fast.

Sura (chapter) VIII of the Quran, entitled "The spoils of War", prescribes in detail the conduct of "Jihad" (holy war) for all time. It has left a brutal imprint on Muslim civilization and morals. The teachings of Jesus of Nazareth could not stand in sharper contrast, although a thousand years after him the crusading nobles from Europe soon imitated the Muslim cruelties when they conquered the "Holy Land" and Jerusalem; hence the Muslim title of "Crusaders" for western leaders.

But while in modern times the rules of war have improved the lot of prisoners of war and wounded enemies in most western countries, Muslim war morals have changed little from the time of Mohammed. The revolting TV images of the beheading of Daniel Pearl, the mean 9/11 attacks on civilians, the ambushes and the suicide vests in Iraq, worn even by women, the child soldiers, the Muslim slave trade in the Sudan and the butchery by Saddam Hussein, all of this and more shows the wide moral gap between East and West.

New fire fighting methods for high rises

Much has been said about the possibility of preventing the 9/11 attacks; allusions being made to warnings received by government officials, fingers pointed and hearings held, but nothing could be certified as fact. The stark truth was that the insurgents' modus operandi was so innovative, so unprecedented and so stealthy that the element of surprise was total. Compared with our ever recurring, unpreventable bank robberies, who could guess the secret machinations of a small Islamic group that was able to roam freely between continents?

To reduce the damage to high rises like the twin towers, the author, in discussions with others, suggested that every large city should have some heavy fire fighting helicopters. If a steady stream of foam could have been directed at the flaming floors, the weakening of the steel beams might have been prevented and many lives saved. Movable slides, heavy ropes and gloves should be standard equipment in situ; soft-concussion "foam bombs" could be invented that can be shot through the windows; large tarpaulins should be available to catch jumping people.

To see those brave firefighters on TV slowly dragging their heavy loads up those unending stairs was heartrending.

Trust weapons in the hands of good Americans

To get back to the question: "What agency is to be blamed for the 9/11 attacks?" The clearest answer is: indiscriminate government control of a free people not allowed to carry firearms for self-protection in deadly situations. All the passengers and pilots aboard the four planes were unarmed. The insurgents had free play. There are all kinds of deadly weapons on the streets of America, secretly carried by criminals, but in a deadly threat no one can defend him or herself at the most critical moment. America has disarmed its people, especially its good people. Those who, as responsible, capable, levelheaded citizens should have been allowed to carry their weapon aboard for an emergency, could easily have shot the five terrorists in each plane (one had four) who stormed the cockpits. Any trained person with a good record could have shot at a terrorist instead of at the fuselage or at other passengers. The repressive gun-laws in North America have created a situation where only criminals and the police carry arms anymore.

Compounding that mistake, the government hit back with expensive Air Marshals and more harassing security measures everywhere. Just to be able to detect a few dozen Muslim insurgents in a country of 300 million, these new police controls make American society harsher. Is it the slippery slope towards totalitarianism, which is defined as total subservience to the state? The whole shemozzle (Hebrew for 'no luck') comes down to the slogan: "In the government we trust, but the government does not trust us". It sounds almost ready for incorporation in the Constitution.

I am not a rifleman, nor even a hunter, but it is easy to see that the more a citizen's traditional freedoms are nibbled away by the government, the less safe America becomes.

As to the international situation, by deciding to wage tidy wars for just ends with conventional methods and within politically and diplomatically correct limits, the U.S. has set the pace for a never-ending, increasingly costly Global War on Terrorism. Unlike Hitler, Osama is patient. Patience and constancy in jihad run like a scarlet thread through the fabric of the Quran. For a few days after 9/11, the terrorists waited and worried about the reprisal that did not come, then they laughed and celebrated. And eventually they will win, because America is too soft in its responses and too naïve in its strategy to make the wily moves that can win the war on terrorism.

Moments of remembrance

I remember attending the first anniversary of the World Trade Center disaster—in 2002. An eerie silence hung over the multitudes, hardly a word was spoken, and the reverence and sorrow were palpable. Untold thousands were lined up for hours, hoping to get a glimpse of the President, but his motorcade sped by without acknowledging the mourners. There were loudspeakers at the corners of ground zero, ostensibly connected to the podium inside, but not a word of solace came through from the President. How easily he could have said that he shared the grief of all that stood outside and waited.

As I drove out of Manhattan late in the evening in light traffic, a sudden flurry of police motorcycles and official cars rushed by me on both sides and, for a belated moment, I sensed the comforting presence of the President, firmly ensconced in his seat.

2.   IRAQ, KEY TO AN ISLAMIC SEA-CHANGE

Who is the real enemy in Iraq?

Many Americans have been blindsided by the idea that the War in Iraq was illegal because of the false W.M.D. motive, resulting in the unnecessary deaths of American soldiers.

But in the previous chapter I hope I showed that the invasion of Iraq was also a masterstroke. I should add that maybe it was unintentionally so, arising out of an instinctive strategic need to establish a strong U.S. presence in the Middle East, no matter where, to counter the rising Islamist threat that deeply affected American soil. The reader will remember that the U.S. singled out three terrorist states (the Axis of Evil), ending with the choice of war on Iraq over Iran and North Korea. Subsequent events in Iraq got Al Qaida pre-occupied in its own neck of the woods and out of the hair of the American population.

We know therefore that those of the American troops in Iraq that fell in battle, died for the safety of the American people and the whole world, as well as for the urgently needed, strategic ends in the entire Middle East. We hope the N. A. T. O. countries realize and appreciate this more and more.

The undeniable, sad truth is that the War in Iraq has been in a stalemate for several years. Negativists like a weak, crying Murtha who look no farther than the length of their noses, are doing the American war effort great harm. Had his antics not been so childish and naïve, they could have been close to treason. Those that screamed for an immediate pullout have no idea that Iraq may be the key to the solution of all future dealings with terrorism, as I will show shortly in this chapter. An immediate withdrawal would be a costly defeat, damaging the U.S. status of superpower and defender of the free West.

Let us look for a minute at the good results the U.S. effort in Iraq has already achieved, because they form the basis on which, through a devious change in its course, the American ship of state can sail to victory.

In the first place, of course: the ouster of a dangerous megalomaniac—of incalculable benefit to the whole world.

Second, as already mentioned: the U.S. knife in the heart of a dangerously hostile part of the globe is an aspect bedeviling Al Qaida's goals in the Middle East.

Third: the war gave bin Laden and associates less time for a new attack on the United States; he only recently got his caves and tunnels repaired, allowing him to go public again.

Fourth: the cave-in of Lybia's strongman Qaddafi.

Fifth: considering the enormous amount of casualties in other U.S. wars—in Europe, the Pacific, Korea and Vietnam—the relatively small number of American heroes that sacrificed their lives for our freedom and the world has been low.

Sixth: Iraq will be a valuable lesson for the U.S. towards its future course of fighting the frontless war on terrorism.

Seventh: a possible new course in Iraq may also lead to better relations with Iran. Iran is not an Arabic country, but a people of Indo-European origin like many of us, with a large percentage of well-educated secular-minded political thinkers; hopefully, Ahmedinejad will soon be a voice of the past.

Eighth: U.S. protection of Iraq's oil wealth will help Iraqi's economy as much as that of the Western user countries.

If America should opt for the Machiavellian shift we will discuss below—the dime on which Iraq can be turned—the U.S. would quickly be able to quit the war with honor (victory) without further loss of life and the further result could be a sea-change in Middle East geopolitics that would greatly benefit the whole free world.

After several years of trying, the United States finally managed to maneuver itself into a position between a rock and a hard place—the rock of American democratic principles and the hard place of Islamic theocratic basics. The Arabic word for base or foundation is "qaida". It bears repeating that it is not just the insurgents that do not want foreign soldiers on their soil. All Quran-believing Muslims moderate or fundamentalist are agreed on this principle.

The ironic fact is that, while both the Shia and the Sunni want the U.S. out on religious grounds, they are also fighting each other on religious grounds. The Sunnis have despised and killed the Shias for centuries. It is here we may find the weakness in the insurgencies that can be exploited. Is this perhaps the KEY to victory in Iraq?

And what kind of victory? Will it result in a democracy in Iraq? A unified Iraq? Will it bring about reconciliation between Shia and Sunni? Would it mean that all U.S. soldiers must leave Iraq right away?

Who in fact is the enemy in Iraq? One day, U.S. troops are fighting Shia insurgents, the next day Sunnis. For every insurgent killed, the U.S. makes scores of enemies, because each is a member of an extended family or clan who mourn the loss of a son, brother, father, uncle, cousin or second cousin; they are all embittered and want REVENGE in accordance with tribal traditions and the Quran. Who is the enemy?

One of the biggest enemies of the United States in Iraq is THE UNITED STATES. By killing both Shias and Sunnis, the U.S. is fighting itself. Such a war cannot be won. It is suicidal. And yet the U.S. must avoid defeat! Defeat for the U.S. is also defeat for the Iraqis.

Anything but victory in Iraq would undo all the previous costly efforts and achievements. It could also cause Islamist revival in Egypt, Saudi-Arabia, Jordan and Turkey, along with renewed threats to Lebanon, Israel, Kashmir, the Sudan and the rest of Africa. No doubt there would also be repercussions in Europe and North America.

Recapitulating, the U.S. can neither "stay the course" in an increasingly unpopular war, nor can it afford to leave.

So, in order to be able to take a new course in Iraq, we must again ask the questions: what is the U.S. fighting for? For democracy in Iraq? Forget it. For reconciliation between old Saddam's Sunnis and the Shias they murdered and whose holy place they destroyed? Impossible.

The answer is, first of all: America should stop being its own enemy. It should realize the futility of pursuing the two false goals of democratization and reconciliation. Secondly, it should determine who the real enemy in Iraq is. That is the key to changing course in Iraq and it has been staring the U.S. in the face for several years.

- Who oppressed the Shias for centuries? The Sunnis.

- Who destroyed the Golden Mosque of Ali? The Sunnis.

- Who continuously sabotaged unity in Iraq? The Sunnis.

- Who walked out of the new government? The Sunnis.

- Who still want control of Iraq's oil? The Sunnis.

- Who are killing U.S. soldiers the most? The Sunnis.

Conclusion: The real enemy of Iraq and America is the Sunni. Therefore, should the U.S. now start fighting the Sunnis? The surprising answer is "No".

The answer is actually quite simple. It is the dagger that can be twisted—it is the ninety-degree shift in the rudder that will allow the American Ship of State to sail around the Islamist cliffs—a pact with the "Devil".

Pact with the Devil

There is only ONE WAY TO WIN THE WAR IN IRAQ: make a pact with the two Shia parties under al-Sadr and al-Maliki. Both would subsequently eliminate the Sunnis and divide the loot. Thousands of Shias were killed by the Sunni Baathists under Saddam Hussein. The U.S. attack on Iraq did not begin as a war on the Shias but on Saddam's Sunnis. The U.S. in effect liberated the Shias. Then it made the foolish mistake of playing the boss over both Sunnis and Shias to force reconciliation and democracy on them, making enemies of both.

The situation is somewhat analogous to the dilemma the Allied forces faced in the war against Hitler Germany. They had to join forces with the murderous communist tyrant Stalin to bring down the sadistic monster Hitler.... They made a pact with the Devil, the Soviet Union. The only huge mistake the Allies made, according to some critics, and which could have saved tens of thousands of Allied casualties, was that the military aid by America to that arch-devil Stalin should have been rationed in such a way that Germany and the Soviet Union would have bled each other to death. It would have been the old story of two dogs fighting over a bone (victory) and the third one running away with it. By not applying the second half of the "divide and rule" trick (the double-dealing), the West was saddled with 45 years of Cold War and a tremendous list of misery, poverty, starvation and death in the huge Soviet Union-controlled part of Europe,

History repeats itself. Once again the West must make a pact with the "Devil", al-Sadr. It is of tremendous strategic advantage to the U.S. to have the two Shia parties each have a roughly equal part of Iraq in peace together by allowing them to get rid of the common enemy, the Sunnis.

If the United States stays firmly in control of the carrot and the stick, it is in a position to win the war by default by allowing the Shias to beat the Sunnis and thus staying out of the struggle. The U.S. would not play an active role in the war on the Sunnis except as an intermediary in the 3-way competition for Iraq's future oil income, because that's what the whole internecine struggle in Iraq is all about.

Instead of wasting billions on the war, the U.S. could promise millions in support of rebuilding Iraq. The U.S. would become a friend of the Shias. Of course, Iran would also figure somewhere in the deal—contextually—but the U.S. would maintain control. It could promise Iran a strong, new Shia bloc, something it wanted all along, in return for all kinds of concessions, especially with regard to the nuclear problem. The U.S. could again become friends with Iran. The U.S. would keep its hands off any further Shia-Sunni hostilities and stand down in bivouac. No more U.S. casualties.

It is clear that, if the Sunnis are chased out of Iraq, it must not result in ethnic cleansing, only insurgent cleansing, similar to King Hussein's action against the Palestinians in 1970. Peaceful Sunnis can stay. The U.N. could initiate a program of helping exiled Sunnis for loss of property and costs of relocation, the end game being Shia security. It is part of a giant struggle between two old rivals that cannot be stopped.

As amply shown above, the Sunni is the real enemy. The armed presence of all Sunnis in Iraq must be eliminated. Failure to root out the Baathist bullies has already cost the U.S. too many lives. Considering past Sunni orientation and behavior, they should have absolutely no meaningful influence in Iraqi politics anymore. In complete contrast, the Sunni Kurds have given the U.S. troops hardly any trouble and have no agenda against the Shias.

A three-way Sistani-Sadr-Kurd political settlement should therefore be possible the role of an al-Maliki or successor would be symbolic, like the Queen of England, with a governor for the Kurds and one each for the two Shia parties or their territory.

The terms under which the three blocs could be united in one government could be roughly summed up as follows:

1) a balance between Muslim and secular rule: Islamic clerical influence, yes—Sharia law only, no;
2) education in all subjects, yes—religious subjects only, no;
3) women's rights, yes—permissive, western style, no;
4) freedom and tolerance in religion, yes, in Islamic context;
5) persecution and debasement of Jews and Christians, no;
6) all future Iraqi oil income to go to Kurds and Shias only, in punishment of the destruction of the sacred Mosque of Ali by the Sunnis on February 22, 2007;
7) an equal number of Kurds and each of the two Shia parties to be elected to a national Union government;
8) the Kurdish northern homeland to include Kirkuk—Turkmen and Arab minorities to be treated humanely;

9) the U.S. to recognize the right of the two Shia parties and the Sunni Kurds to eliminate all hostile Sunni elements from Iraq to prevent future insurrection and interference;

10) the U.S. to retain a base or bases in Iraq to safeguard the oil bases and national security;

11) withdrawal of all U.S. forces to take place at a mutually convenient date.

The time to act is now. I predict that if the U.S. continues to appease the Sunnis, it will be faced with a repeat of Munich 1938 or worse. World War III might become inevitable, weakening the U.S. A strong Iraq-Iran bloc against the Sunnis is essential and may save the West.

The new Shia-Kurd Union of Iraq

The core of the pro-Shia shift would be the total destruction of all Sunni hostile bands in Iraq. Otherwise it is impossible to have a durable peace or a stable Iraq. To try to appease hostile Sunnis only invites further trouble. National borders in Islamic countries do not function like they do in the West, as all Muslim lands are theoretically one under the Umma, the community of believers. Displaced Sunnis can therefore always find refuge in another Islamic country. Furthermore, there should be no more Sunni emigration to the U.S.

The Shias should become a free people again. They have a culture and religious orientation all of their own. In the long run, it is worth strengthening them against their archenemies, the Sunnis.

The name Shia comes from the full name "Shiat Ali", Partisans of Ali. (Shiat is the plural of Shia.) Ali was the son-in-law of the Prophet Mohammed. Ali's descendants, through his wife Fatima, consider themselves the true followers of Mohammed. At one time they were the leading faction but have shrunken through the centuries to less than 20% of the total Muslim population due to persecution by the Sunnis.

Ali was assassinated by a fanatic opponent in the year 661. In the struggle for supremacy, the Shias were defeated by the Sunnis time and again. Untold Shia fathers and grown sons were killed, their wives and children enslaved and forcibly converted to the Sunni faith, a striking example of the lot that befell the Jewish Banu Quraiza tribe and sure evidence of the secret behind the unbelievably quick spread of Islam in the Mediterranean in the course of only a few centuries.

Who can argue that the Shias do not have the right to civil war? No one intervened when America had its own and the outcome was stabilization and a stronger nation, not chaos. The time for Shia freedom has come. At the same time, U.S. soldiers no longer have to lose their lives for a bunch of useless, thankless, merciless Sunnis anymore. All previous attempts to win the hearts of any Muslim nation for western morals and democracy ended in failure. When the Dutch colonized what is now Indonesia in the 1600s, they had to swear that they would not convert the indigenous people to Christianity. The best we can hope for in a new Iraq is stability and a moderate form of government, not a democracy in any Western sense.

And what of a Sunni country like Saudi-Arabia that would protest the new American stance against the Iraqi Sunnis? Would it threaten with oil cuts and even higher gas prices? That would only put America's drive for alternative energy into higher gear and ultimately harm the oil sheiks. Maybe the U.S. should call Saudi Arabia's bluff for once and tell it: "We're done with Iraq and maybe the time has come to put a few hot coals under your feet." In more diplomatic terms it would mean that the U.S. could deal with any new Muslim problem on a new basis once its hands are free in Iraq.

So in conclusion, the desirable policy is neither "staying the course" nor a "walkout deadline". The best solution is turning the rudder and changing the course to a new divide and rule strategy that will save soldiers' lives, lower the obscene cost of war, put the Iraq war in the history books as a qualified victory, enable the U.S. to deploy its forces to other trouble spots, create a new balance of power in the Middle East and apply the lesson of Iraq to future clashes or confrontations with an ever expanding Islamist "front".

3.   ISLAM EXPANDING EVERYWHERE

Pakistan wants Kashmir

Almost all Muslim countries obtaining independence after World War II have lapsed into undemocratic theocracies or tyrannies. One example of a post-colonial state where democracy took firm root is Hindu-Buddhist India, an icon of stability. The only people in India that are causing the most trouble are the Muslims, who oppose India's sovereignty over Kashmir.

Pakistan waged four holy wars with India over Kashmir, a vast territory allotted to India by the U.N. in 1947.

When Afghanistan was fighting the Russian invaders in the 1980s, the United States came to its help because the Soviet presence at that time was still a threat. The U.S. also kept its hands off neighboring Pakistan in its dispute with India over Kashmir, just to keep Pakistan as a friend against the Soviet Union as well—short-term policy, but not entirely inexcusable.

But allowing Pakistan to build the atomic bomb was a colossal, irresponsible long-term lack of vision by the U.S. It further alienated India because its chances of winning the war against Pakistan were weakened and the result was a stalemate, with Pakistan in control of half of Kashmir. It is almost certain that in the long run friendship with Pakistan will hurt the U.S.

When the Soviets left the Middle East in 1989, the U.S. could easily have switched sides and Pakistan could have been crushed between India's superior army and American might.

Again, with the U.S. becoming embroiled in Iraq, a wily Perverz Musharraf must have foreseen the futility of that struggle and politically supported the U.S., because hi strongman rule was being seriously challenged by the Taliban.

If ever the time comes when the religious leaders of Pakistan join the Muslim chorus for the U.S. to get out of the Middle East (and that time may be nearer than we expect), the U.S. will be faced with a new regime in Pakistan that will be hostile to western influences and fully armed with equally hostile nuclear weapons.

Betrayal of Serbia

The American debacle in Serbia' under the Clinton administration was a prime example of short-sighted politics designed to save the "poor Muslims" of Kosovo from the "greedy hands" of Christian Serbia. Did Clinton want the Muslims' respect? Or was it a show-off to the United Nations how mighty America could fix Serbia much faster from the air where the Serbs were defenseless? Did he know he was waging jihad for Allah? Or that he would leave the destabilization problem in the Balkans basically unsolved?

For hundreds of years the Serbs, Bulgarians, Hungarians, Yugoslavs and other Balkan neighbors had been robbed, murdered, enslaved, subjugated and forcibly converted by the Muslims.

Kosovo had always been the heartland of the Serbian Orthodox Church; a peaceful religious group with ancient connections to the Byzantine Church in former Anatolia (now Turkey), until the Muslim Albanian illegals crossed its border.

The U.S. has a similar problem with illegal Mexicans, but at least those people are a factor in peacefully building America, whereas the Muslim invaders, multiplying through their high birthrate, became the majority in Kosovo and then, in often savage murder and looting became its de facto masters. Now they want independence from the Serbian Christian "dogs".

It appears that Europe's history is being rewritten: there is little cause to believe that the Muslims will not cause more problems in all of Europe.

What did the U.S. gain by punishing the Serbs for trying to kick the Albanians out of their cuckoos' nests and retaking their old, sacred homelands and properties in Kosovo? Had not enough Balkan blood been spilled by the Muslims through the centuries?

One could question if it was all right for America to take Florida, Texas, New Mexico, Arizona and most of California from Mexico. At least the 1803 Louisiana Purchase from Napoleon was a deal, the same as the purchase of Alaska. But it was all for a bigger country and what is the difference between a greater America and a greater Serbia? The latter term was frequently in the news, although the media knew darn well that Kosovo was still a part of what was left of Yugoslavia and not a new acquisition for a greater Serbia.

Was it right for the U.S. to kill and expel the Indians but wrong for the Serbs to get rid of the bandit Muslims that had been waging a war of terror against the Serbs, riling them to the limit? Although the Serbs' methods were harsh, their leader, Milosevich, was the only strongman who could have restored long-term unity and stability in Yugoslavia, giving back to the Orthodox Church its holy sites and population.

Taken to The Hague for war crimes against the terrorists, Milosevich died in jail, mostly of grief. Many Americans felt that Serbia should have been given more time towards democracy.

Did the Kosovo Muslims help the U.S. in Iraq in reverent thankfulness? Deep in their hearts they are convinced that America simply did Allah's will in bombing the Serbs into submission. Muslim gratitude and goodwill towards the West are as amazing and impressive as a tooth fairy's gift.

At the time the U.S. did its bombing, only fifty percent of the American people were in favor of it, yet Clinton in his stridency went where the cautious Europeans participating in the Balkan military action feared to tread. When prudence should have been the watchword, Clinton escalated his "punitive" raids. At first, these were restricted to military objectives only, as had been agreed on. Then Clinton decided to amplify the attacks by bombing civilian targets like bridges and railroad stations, and when that was not enough, he ordered the destruction of electrical installations. About 3,000 Serbian civilians were killed, roughly the same as in 9/11. This bizarre coincidence was probably not lost on some Americans and Serbians.

The bombings were not a mistake, but a war crime—and against E.U. high staff orders. Being directed at a small, defenseless country, they were also callous and cowardly.

Like Milosevich, why was Clinton not summoned to The Hague to answer for this carnage and destruction? Why did he do this for the Albanians who had the help of many Islamist jihad warriors from all over the Muslim world? Why play the harlot with bin Laden?

The Kosovo thing was way bigger than a petty tyrant. It affected the future of the whole Balkan Peninsula. Many Americans were of the opinion that Serbia should have been given more time towards democracy.

For more insight into the Clinton years, the reader is referred to *The Final Days* by Barbara Olson and *The Death of Outrage* by William J. Bennett. But good luck to Hillary

What should be done about Kosovo? It should never be recognized as an independent state by the United Nations.

It has always been an integral part of Serbia and should stay so. Kosovo is now part of the Muslim threat to Europe that is becoming more acute each decade.

Darfur, another Muslim assault

Why does the U.S. sit and watch the genocide in the Sudan as though it is not urgent? Almost a million people, Christians and pagans, have been murdered by the Janjaweed with consent of the Sudanese Muslim government and about two million have been driven from their homes. Europe is not stopping this ancient vicious method of Muslim expansion either. Is the civilized world not yet aware of the growing Muslim dominance everywhere? Part of the answer? The U.S. is tied up in the Middle East.

Ethiopia, the Philippines, Lebanon
(more Muslim expansion)

The statistics tell us these are countries where former Muslim minorities have been expanding to half or more of the Christian population (Ethiopia and Lebanon) or where Muslims have the majority in a segment of the country (The Philippines) through higher birth rates.

All three are faced with a future marked by incessant Muslim fighting for sharia law. There will never be peace until that goal has been reached, no matter how much bloodshed or other cruelties it takes. With the introduction of sharia law, these countries will lose their former freedoms of religion, education, the press etc., in brief we may say, their civilization.

Fifty years ago, Ethiopia was an overwhelmingly Christian nation, with roots going back to the beginning of

Christianity. Now, the Muslim part of the population has reached 50% and the doom of the Christian Church may soon be sealed.

The prospect in Lebanon and The Philippines is also one of never-ending Muslim strife. In the end, Islam always wins.

Naive anti-colonialism

The post-World War II decolonization process went much .too fast. Although it was a factor in shooting the U.S. to world power heights, many new nations were not ready to govern themselves and now have the status of "failed".

Had we given England, France and The Netherlands, the three colonial empires, as well as Belgium, Spain and Portugal, a free hand in smoothing the transition from colony to independence, the U.S. would have had the help of several European nations policing an unruly world of neophytes. This is especially relevant to Muslim and part-Muslim nations such as Eritrea, Ethiopia, the Sudan and, Zambia in Africa as well as in several Middle East locations where Sunni clerics are striving hard to bring their followers back to the pristine seventh century in a universal (Umma) context. This movement could be called IMMURE, an acronym for Implementing Muslim Resurgence.

Furthermore, it appears that the U.S. and the Soviet Union should never have interfered with the Anglo-French intervention in the Suez Canal in 1956, nor should the Israelis have been forced out of the Sinai Peninsula at the time. The Sinai could have become a homeland for the thousands of displaced Jews from Syria, Iran and other places. That would have created a large buffer zone with. Egypt, while simultaneously the Suez Canal could have been

37

put under international supervision. President Eisenhower's administration did not have the stamina and foresight to call the Russians' bluff at the time, unlike President Kennedy did later during the Cuban missile crisis, when the Soviet Union had become much stronger. The above examples all show a lack of long-term vision.

As it was, the U.S. anti-colonial policy weakened Europe, beginning in 1947 through 1950, when both India (Great Britain) and Indonesia (The Netherlands) became independent; French Vietnam followed in 1955, the Sudan in 1956 and the Belgian Congo in 1960 – to mention some of the important initial rollovers. The latter two are extremely unstable.

In a little over a decade Great Britain had been reduced from world power to a medium state. So here we see the face of Europe changing, losing almost all of its overseas possessions.

A total of 126 new U.N. members firmed up between 1944 and 1994. It is worth noting that about 50 of these are either Muslim or under strong Muslim pressure, becoming an increasingly strong voice in the world body and bound to outvote the West at some future time.

The rudder shift

To neutralize and diminish the power of rogue Islamist countries in the United Nations, the U.S. should become more cynical in its dealings with the Middle East, using the dagger of divide and rule more and more instead of brute military power. This should enable it to devote more time to endangered ethnic groups with western leanings such as in Armenia, Ethiopia, Lebanon, the Philippines, the Sudan and other trouble spots.

Former Russian Armenia needs special consideration. Perhaps in return for the 1915-1916 genocide of over a million Armenians by the Turks and Kurds, the land-locked nation should be given a corridor to the Black Sea. The Turks should be given the bitter pill of either acknowledging the genocide, (something they obstinately, refuse to do) or give land or the use of land as goodwill. If the Kurds would be willing to atone for the past and assist Armenia, they might have a better chance of getting something out of it for themselves as well. The Machiavellian screws could be tightened by an anonymous "suggestion" to divide Turkey between Greece, Kurdistan and Armenia. While this could begin as a paper game to rile or scare the Turks, it would be instructive to at least see what reactions, such as troop movements or counter threats, would ensue.

In retrospect the Allies should have cut up Turkey in 1918. Be that as it may, the U.S. or Russia should be able to assess the situation and arm the Kurds and Armenians for defensive purposes. Turkey is becoming an Islamist enemy—the future will bear this out. As a note, the 1994 win by Armenia in Nagorno-Karabakh at the expense of Azerbaijan is proof that the Armenians are terrific fighters against terrorists.

The main idea behind all this is not war, but a bit of "meaning teasing" by the U.S. and Russia to have Turkey make at least some repairs for their genocide during World War I. The pressure could be augmented by veiled threats of support for the Armenians, Kurds and Greeks in their still valid claims for the return of the vast amounts of property stolen in 1915.

America should enlist the help of these three enemies of Turkey. It cannot police the world alone. It keeps getting bogged down in expensive, fruitless wars against small bands of terrorist fanatics. Why not shift its global policy from one of democracy-building to "smart war tricks" of divide and rule? The doctrine of preemptive attack and the classic army, navy and air force combat, based on illusions, will ultimately fail in the war on religious terrorism and too many fronts, sapping the U.S. economy, causing loss of public support and possibly a debacle.

It would make more sense to become friends with Russia again, investing in its oil production and start importing more oil from Russia and Canada and less from the Middle East. At the same time it could support the Russians' struggles against Muslim troublemakers on a common ideological and strategic basis.

China is a different type of dinosaur. Would it take a giant Machiavellian effort to bring it to its knees and give up on either Taiwan or Tibet? There is a very effective and cheap method to do this, but I had to seal and leave it at one of my lawyers.

U.S. failure to react instantly after 9/11 and the years-long impasse in the Middle East has impeded its leverage on the rest of the world. As a result, it is has to play along with the incredibly slow U.N. process of caution, diplomacy and sanctions. This is not a chance phenomenon. The same U.N. did nothing in Rwanda as one million Tutsis were butchered.

Also, Europe is being coddled by Al Qaida to distance it from the U.S. The exceptions are Britain and Spain, but Al Qaida uses the carrot and the stick quite adroitly. The bombings in Britain and Spain were a warning to other European countries.

Al Qaida (which is definitely present in Europe) has a policy of withholding direct fire at Europe, concentrating its violent energy on the U.S. invaders of Muslim lands. The result is a European mentality of doubt regarding the U.S. venture in Iraq, resulting in small contributions of arms and personnel. It is as if the Europeans are saying: "If you were not so hard on those poor Muslims and did not try to push your ideas on the Middle East so much, the Muslims would treat you a lot better".

Al Qaida will continue to be soft on Europe, in fact applying the "divide and rule" principle against the U.S. It is sucking the U.S. deeper into a crazy triangular war in Iraq while playing footsie with Europe.

If the U.S. cannot or will not unsnarl itself and does not twist the dagger, it is lost.

The pain of terror is a horrible strain
and if President B. O. can't stop the Muslim train
his reign will be in vain.

4. JIHAD–FIGHTING IN THE WAY OF ALLAH

War against Jews and Christians

This chapter is designed to show from the actual texts in the Quran that every Muslim believer has the God-given duty to kill Jews and Christians in holy war (jihad). The texts have not been selected haphazardly, but in the context of the regularly recurring theme of Jihad. Unlike the Bible, the Quran does not have extended prose descriptions of events. Most texts deal with one revealed phrase in a couple of lines. Muslims believe that each text was verbally delivered to Mohammed by the angel of Allah, to be recited (said aloud) and memorized.

Some Western apologists maintain that the word "jihad" can mean inner, spiritual struggle but that is very rare. The reader will soon catch on that all references to jihad are warlike, anchored in the phrase "fighting in the way of Allah".

The word *mujahideen* means fighter in Holy War. It is clear from the following excerpts that jihad is the duty of every able-bodied Muslim. The highest peak of faith a Muslim can reach is to fall in battle for Allah. It means instant entry into Heaven, whereas all others must wait till the Day of Judgment. At that time the latter will find out if their good deeds measure up against the bad ones as Allah and His angels are weighing them on a scale.

Sura (Chapter) 9:88-89 says: *"But the Apostle and those who believe with him strive hard with their property and their persons; and these it is who shall have all the good things and they are the ones who shall be successful. Allah has prepared for them gardens wherein rivers flow, to remain in them, their great reward. There is also a reward for all who shelter and feed the combatants"*.

This means that in Iraq today those that shelter and feed the insurgents (the ones planting bombs for example) shall also have their reward from Allah. Incidentally, if an insurgent is caught going into his shelter and the shelter provider is shot by a U.S. soldier in a fight, he is counted as a terrorist by the Americans, but as a civilian by his fellow-Iraqis. It is the moral duty of every Muslim believer to kill the enemies of Allah "wherever he finds them" and the killing of such an enemy is no different from killing an animal. To a Muslim, a Christian is a dog.

Typical examples from the Prophet's life illustrate this nonchalant attitude toward the enemy of Allah. When Mohammed had consolidated his position at Medina after the Battle of Badr in 624, he decided to get rid of some of his detractors. A Jew named Kab ibn al-Ashraf that was writing nasty poetry about the Prophet, inciting the Meccans against him, was one of them. After luring him into a trap, Mohammed's helpers cut off his head and threw it down at the feet of the Prophet the next morning. Mohammed praised them for their good work "in the way of Allah".

A certain poetess named Asma bint Marwan also wrote bitter, ribald verse against Mohammed. "Can no one get rid of this woman for me?" the Prophet cried. One of his disciples slipped into the woman's dwelling that night, carefully lifted the baby from her breast and stabbed her to death. Meeting Mohammed at his headquarters, he asked if he had to worry about eternal consequences. "Not a bit", answered the Prophet, "it's no worse than killing a goat".

There was also a gentler, even generous side to the Prophet and he could be a real diplomat if it suited him. From what I read about the amicable behavior of Osama bin Laden among own people, the similarity between the two men is so striking that they could have been brothers. Both could be incredibly cruel and ruthless in the pursuit of their vision of a new world-order. But unlike despots like Stalin, Hitler and Saddam Hussein who all had streaks of paranoia that caused them to mistrust everybody, Mohammed and bin Laden share a religious energy, augmented by military cunning and financial success that attract capable, trustworthy followers.

Bin Laden's organization may ultimately turn out to be a much greater challenge to Western civilization than any loopy secular tyrant who has to instill loyalty with the gun. Of course, bin Laden's approach is completely out of sync with today's Western concepts of the dignity and potential of each human being regardless of religious creed. Present-day Islamists are still laboring under the 1400-year old maxims that they think must some day prevail over the whole world.

To clear away any doubt whether the ultimate aim of converting the whole world is held only by the Islamists, the author has reproduced from the Quran almost all relevant passages which oblige every single Muslim in the world to fight in the Way of Allah when called to do so. The reason American Muslims do not fight in the Way of Allah as yet is that they are under clerical orders to remain patient until the time is ripe. This could be anywhere from 25 to 50 years away or it could be sooner. Later in the book, I will offer some remedies for this uncertainty about a Muslim's ultimate loyalty as citizen.

The Quran is divided into 114 suras, or chapters, with verses (sayings) of varying length. The second half of the book is the oldest and the more peaceful, written before Mohammed fell out with the Jews and Christians.

The jihad verses reproduced here give a clear insight into the mind of Mohammed and today's Muslim beliefs.

The Jihad verses:

Sura	Verse	
2	80	ALLAH'S CURSE IS ON THE UNBELIEVERS.
	111	They say: None shall enter Paradise unless he is a Jew or a Christian. How vain they are. Tell them: If you are right, bring your proof.
	113	The Jews say: The Christians do not follow the right path and the Christians say: The Jews do not follow the right path and both recite from the same Book. So Allah shall judge between them on the Day of Judgment.
	135	They say: Be Jews or Christians and you will be on the right Path. Tell them: NO, OURS IS THE RELIGION OF ABRAHAM, the Hanif who did not believe in more than one God.
	190	FIGHT IN THE WAY OF ALLAH against those who fight you, not exceeding the limits, for Allah does not love those that exceed the limits.
	191	AND KILL THEM WHEREVER YOU FIND THEM AND DRIVE THEM OUT FROM WHERE THEY DROVE YOU OUT WITH AN INTENSITY SEVERE IN SLAUGHTER, but do not fight them at the Sacred Mosque, unless they fight you there; if they do fight you there, kill them, such are the wages of the unbeliever.

192 But if they desist, Allah is forgiving, merciful.

193 Otherwise, FIGHT THEM UNTIL THERE IS NO MORE OPPOSITION AND RELIGION IS ONLY FOR ALLAH. Again, if they desist, war shall cease except against those who press on.

216 FIGHTING IS YOUR DUTY, even if you dislike it. You might well dislike something that is good for you, or love something that is bad for you, but Allah knows what you do no know.

244 FIGHT IN THE WAY OF ALLAH; know that Allah hears and knows.

3   151 (Allah says) WE WILL STRIKE TERROR INTO THE HEARTS OF THE UNBELIEVERS, who have a god besides Allah against His will: their abode shall be in the fire. Evil is the abode of the unjust.

4   74 Those who FIGHT IN THE WAY OF AL LAH, sell this world's life for the hereafter and whoever FIGHTS IN ALLAH'S WAY, whether he be slain or victorious, we shall grant him a mighty reward.

76 Those who believe FIGHT IN THE WAY OF ALLAH and those who do not believe fight in the way of Satan. Fight therefore against the friends of Satan; surely Satan's strategy is weak.

84	FIGHT THEN IN ALLAH'S WAY, you yourselves and those whose zeal you arouse. Maybe Allah will hold back the fighting of the unbelievers.

84   FIGHT THEN IN ALLAH'S WAY, you yourselves and those whose zeal you arouse. Maybe Allah will hold back the fighting of the unbelievers.

95   Those of the believers who stay in the rear with no injury and those who STRIVE HARD IN ALLAH'S WAY with their property and persons are unequal. ALLAH holds those who strive with their property and persons far above those who keep back. Allah has promised something for each, but he will give the fighters a much higher re ward than those who tarry.

104   AND BE NOT WEAKHEARTED IN PURSUIT OF THE ENEMIES. If you suffer pain, so will they, and you have a hope from Allah and they have none. Allah knows and is wise.

160   So for the iniquity of those who are Jews and for holding back many from Allah's Way did We hold back from them the good things that had been lawfully theirs.

161   Also for taking interest, although they had been forbidden it, and for falsely taking people's property have we prepared a painful punishment for those unbelievers.

5   17   Also those are unbelievers who say: ALLAH IS THE MESSIAH, THE SON OF MARY, his mother

33   The punishment of those who fight against Allah and His Apostle and strive to make trouble in our land is this: THEY SHALL

BE MURDERED OR HANGED or their hands and feet cut off on opposite sides or imprisoned. That shall be their shame in this world, and in the hereafter they shall get a severe punishment.

51   Oh you who believe; DO NOT TAKE THE JEWS AND THE CHRISTIANS AS FRIENDS; they are each other's friends. If any of you takes one of them as a friend he is surely one of them; Allah will not be a guide to the faithless.

54   Oh you who believe! Whenever some of you turn back from their religion, surely Allah can raise up a people whom He will love and who will love Him in obedience as believers and who will be STRONG AGAINST THE UNBELIEVERS; THEY WILL STRIVE HARD IN ALLAH'S WAY and shall not fear.

72   Surely they are unbelievers who say: Allah is the Messiah, the son of Mary, whereas the Messiah said: Children of Israel serve Allah, my Lord and your Lord.

73   Surely they are unbelievers who say: Allah is the third of three; there is no god but the one God and if they do not stop saying that, a severe punishment will await those who believe that.

116   Allah will say: Oh Jesus, son of Mary, did you say to men: Take me and my mother for two Gods besides Allah? He will answer: Glory be to Thee. It would not be seemly to say what I would not have any right to say.

8	12	The lord said to the angels: I am with you, make the believers steadfast AND I WILL CAST TERROR INTO THE HEARTS OF THE UNBELIEVERS. SO CUT OFF THEIR HEADS AND FINGERTIPS.
	13	Because they opposed Allah and his Apostle. And whoever opposes Allah and his Apostle, Allah will surely punish him severely.
	14	They will find out that unbelievers will be punished in the fire.
	15	Oh you who believe! When you meet those who disbelieve marching against you in war, do not turn your back.
	16	Whoever turns his back to them on that day, unless he does so for valid reasons or to join another company, will surely deserve Allah's wrath and he will suffer in hell, a terrible destination.
	17	FOR IT IS NOT YOU WHO SLEW THEM BUT ALLAH AND YOU DID NOT STRIKE THEM BUT ALLAH DID and he will confer on the believers a great reward. Allah hears and knows.
	18	Not only that. Allah is the one who WEAKEN THE STRUGLLE OF THE UNBELIEVERS.
	22	Surely the VILEST OF ANIMALS IN ALLAH'S SIGHT are those who dishonor Him.
	38	Tell those who disbelieve that if they stop fighting everything in the past will be forgiven them, but if they come back they

will get what happened to those before them.

39 AND FIGHT THEM UNTIL THERE IS NO MORE OPPOSITION AND THE RELIGION IS ONLY FOR ALLAH. But if they stop, Allah will see if they are sincere.

50 Have you seen how the angels caused the unbeliever to die, when they lit him in the face and on the back saying: Here, take the fire of punishment.

55 SURELY THE VILEST OF ANIMALS IN THE SIGHT OF ALLAH ARE THE UNBELIEVERS.

56 And as to those with whom you made an agreement and then they break it all the time and do not keep it,

57 when you overtake them in fighting then hit them in the back for a reminder.

58 And if you suspect betrayal by some, then treat them the same way. Allah does not love the treacherous.

59 DO NOT LET THE UNBELIEVERS THINK THEY CAN WIN; THEY WILL NOT SUCCEED.

60 And prepare against them any armor you can...and whatever you will spend IN ALLAH'S WAY, it will be fully paid back; you will not be treated unjustly.

61 And if they want to make peace, then grant it and trust Allah. He hears and knows all.

62 And if they intend to deceive you, Allah will advise you. He will strengthen and help you and all the believers.

65 Oh Prophet, URGE THE BELIEVERS TO
    WAR; IF THERE ARE TWENTY CALM
    ONES AMONGST YOU THEY WILL
    OVERCOME TWO HUNDRED and if
    there are a hundred, they will overcome a
    thousand because the unbelievers are
    not wily.

66 At times Allah has to lighten your burdens
    for He knows your little strength, so
    IF THERE ARE HUNDRED PATIENT
    ONES AMONGST YOU, THE WILL
    OVERCOME TWO HUNDRED and if
    there are a thousand, they will overcome
    two thousand, Allah willing. Allah is with
    those who are patient.

67 It is not fit for a prophet that he should take
    any prisoners unless HE HAS FIRST
    SLAUGHTERED IN THE LAND. You
    want the frail booty of this world, But Allah
    wants you to gain the hereafter. Allah is
    mighty and wise.

72 Surely those who believed and ran out and
    FOUGHT HARD IN ALLAH'S WAY with
    their property and their souls and THOSE
    WHO GAVE SHELTER AND HELPED,
    they are the ones that form a team together.

74 And those who believed and ran out and
    FOUGHT HARD IN ALLAH'S WAY and
    those WHO GAVE SHELTER AND
    HELPED, they are the true believers they
    shall have forgiveness and an honorable
    reward.

9   5   When the sacred months have passed, SLAY THE IDOLATORS WHEREVER YOU FIND THEM, and TAKE THEM CAPTIVE and BESIEGE THEM and LIE IN AMBUSH FOR THEM and then, if they repent and observe the prayers and pay the poor-rate, leave them alone: Allah is forgiving and merciful.

12   And if they break their oaths after their agreement and revile your religion, then FIGHT THE LEADER OF UNBELIEF so they may desist; their oaths mean nothing

14   FIGHT THEM, ALLAH WILL PUNISH THEM BY YOUR HANDS and bring them to shame and help you against them and mend the hearts of the believers.

29   FIGHT THOSE WHO DO NOT BELIEVE IN ALLAH nor in the Last Day, who do not forbid what Allah and his Apostle have forbidden NOR FOLLOW THE RELIGION OF TRUTH, even those who have been given the Book, until they pay the Tax in obedience to our superiority and their state of subjection.

30   The Jews say: EZRA IS THE SON OF ALLAH and the Christians say: THE MESSIAH IS THE SON OF ALLAH; those are their vain words, the same as were said by the unbelievers before them. MAY ALLAH DESTROY THEM, how errant they became!

31   They have taken their doctors of law and monks as authorities on Allah and MADE

THE MESSIAH SON OF MARY EQUAL TO ALLAH even though they were told to serve one God only. There is no God but Allah and far from his glory is anyone they make Equal to him.

32   He is the One who sent his Apostle with guidance and THE RELIGION OF TRUTH that he might cause it TO PREVAIL OVER ALL RELIGIONS, although those who worship more than one God may oppose Us.

36   Therefore FIGHT THOSE WHO HAVE MORE THAN ONE GOD like they fight you. Know that Allah is with those who guard against evil.

38   Oh you who believe; .when you were told to GO FORTH IN ALLAH'S WAY, why did you cling to your earthly goods? Are you satisfied with only this world's life instead of the hereafter? What you gain from this life is but little compared to the hereafter.

39   IF YOU DO NOT GO FORTH WE WILL PUNISH YOU with a severe punishment and replace you with another people without it causing Allah any harm. Allah is all Powerful.

41   Whether light or heavy, GO FORTH AND FIGHT IN ALLAH'S WAY WITH YOUR PROPERTY AND YOUR PERSONS. Know that such is better for you.

	123	Oh you who believe, FIGHT THE UNBELIEVERS near you and LET THEM FIND HARDNESS IN YOU. Know that Allah is with those who guard against evil.
22	39	PERMISSION TO FIGHT IS GIVEN TO THOSE UPON WHOM WAR IS MADE because they are oppressed. Most surely Allah is able to help them.
	78	AND STRIVE HARD IN ALLAH'S WAY for striving is due to Him. He has chosen you and has not laid upon you a difficult religion, the faith of Abraham.
25	52	So do not follow the unbelievers but STRIVE AGAINST THEM WITH ALL YOUR MIGHT.
29	6	And whoever STRIVES HARD ONLY FOR HIS SOUL, most surely Allah is self-sufficient, far above this world.
47	4	So when you meet in battle those who disbelieve, CUT THEIR THROATS UNTIL YOU HAVE OVERCOME THEM, then make prisoners and afterwards either release them as a favor or let them pay ransom until the war is over…
48	16	Say to the desert people who were left behind: YOU WILL: SOON BE CALLED UP AGAINST A PEOPLE POSSESSING MIGHTY POWER: FIGHT THEM

UNTIL THEY SUBMIT and if they obey, Allah will reward you richly, but if you turn back as you TURNED BACK BEFORE, He will punish you severely.

57   10   And for what reason should you not SPEND IN ALLAH'S WAY? From Allah is the inheritance of the heavens and the earth. THOSE WHO SPENT AND FOUGHT before victory are not like others. They are more exalted in rank than those who spent and fought afterwards. Allah has promised good to all but Allah is aware of what you do.

59   2   Allah had caused some of THE PEOPLE OF THE BOOK WHO DISBELIEVED € to flee the first time they were banished. They thought that their fortresses would protect them against Allah but He came to them unexpectedly AND CAST TERROR INTO THEIR HEARTS.

60   1   Oh you who believe. Do not take My enemy and your enemy as friends. Would you offer them your love while they deny what you have received as the Truth? Driving out the Apostle and yourselves because you believe in Allah your Lord? IF YOU GO FORTH FIGHTING HARD IN MY PATH and seeking my pleasure would you show love to them?

61	4	Surely ALLAH LOVES THOSE WHO FIGHT IN HIS WAY IN RANKS as if they were a solid wall.
	11	You shall believe in Allah and His Apostle and FIGHT HARD IN ALLAH'S WAY WITH YOUR PROPERTY AND YOUR LIVES.
66	9	Oh Prophet, FIGHT HARD AGAINST THE UNBELIEVERS AND THE HYPO-CRITES AND BE HARD AGAINST THEM. Their abode will be in hell, an evil resort.

Islamic beginnings

The Arabic words for fighting (or striving) in the Way of Allah are "jihad fi sabil Allah". It does not have an inner, spiritual meaning. Bin Laden's method of fighting jihad totally belies that idea. It is nothing else than armed conflict with the unbelievers to gain world supremacy for Islam.

In the Quran this warfare is directed against Christians and Jews, but the term "unbelievers" automatically includes followers of Hinduism, Buddhism and other religions, as well as secularism, agnosticism, indigenous beliefs and, of course, atheism. American non-religious free-thinkers who tout Islam as a peaceful "ideology" would be the first to feel the hard stroke of the jihadist's blade on their necks, if ever America became Muslim.

It is interesting to note that the Arabic Muslims are Semitic and speak a language closely related to Hebrew, very similar to the relationship between Spanish and Italian. The

Arabic word "Allah" and Hebrew "El" go back thousands of years to the same Semitic root. Arabic "mai" for water is Hebrew "mayim" (poetic plural), Hebrew "midrash" is related to Arabic "madrassah", "shen" to "sinn" (tooth), 'rosh' to "ra's" (head), "quds" to "qadesh" (sanctuary), "loh" to "laa" (no) etc.

The Arabs take great offense at the Christian dogma of Jesus being the Son of God. However, every Christian knows that Jesus was not a son in the crude physical sense, but that he was a Son in a spiritual sense because God is perceived as a Spirit. Hence, when Christians refer to themselves as "children of God" or call God "our Father" in prayer, they use strictly spiritual terms to imply closeness to God.

When Muslims call America "The Great Satan", they know full well they are making an exaggerated comparison.

Mohammed's main accusation against the Jews was of having two Gods, viz. El and Uzayr (Ezra). Did that refer to Eleazar whom the Jews revered as the hero of Masada? It means "God has helped", not El = Azar. Most scholars agree the reference is to a man named Ezra in the Bible book with the same title, namely Ezra, the priest (see Ezra 7). And in Ezra 7:1-5 we find a 16-generation genealogical lineage of purely human ancestors of Ezra going back to Aaron (Haroun in Arabic). To the Jews, no Ezra was ever a god.

The answer to this puzzle is typically Islamic, as follows: since Mohammed received everything that is written in the Quran from the angel of Allah, all Jewish and Christian writings preceding or following those revelations that differ from the Quranic revelations are considered distortions! Muslim legalists contend that Allah in His all-encompassing Wisdom gave His final, unchangeable Revelation to the Prophet Mohammed.

For instance, Muslims deny that there ever was a Jewish Temple on the spot in Jerusalem where now stands the Al Aqsa Mosque (the Haram-as-Sharif) This in spite of the detailed account in the Book of Ezra, which documents the difficulties experienced by the Jews in rebuilding the Temple during the reigns in Persia of Artaxerxes, Cyrus and Darius.

By postulating Ezra as a "god", equal to Allah, the Quranic message seems to distance itself from the whole temple-rebuilding story. Similarly, the frequent mentions in the Bible of Jesus going to the Temple in Jerusalem find no mention in the Quran. In his references to Jesus (Isa in Arabic), Mohammed never refers to the Jewish Temple. On the other hand, we have the independent source of Josephus, a near contemporary of Jesus, who described the destruction of the Temple in 70 A.D. in vivid detail. It does not appear that Mohammed ever ordered the building of the Al Aqsa Mosque in Jerusalem either.

The most telling refutation of any polytheism on the part of the Jews is the emphatic Hebrew "Shema Yisrael, Adonai Elohenu Adonai Echad" (Hear Oh Israel, the Lord our God, our Lord is One"). It is endorsed by Jesus as the foremost commandment (Mark 12:29a), omitted in Matthew and Luke.

The corresponding Islamic proclamation "La ilaha illa Llahu" (Sura 5:73, above)—"There is no God but Allah", is so strikingly close to the Hebrew formula in brevity, content and impact as to point to Jewish provenance. Since it was Mohammed's initial plan to win the Jews and Christians over, it seems logical that he was acquainted with the Jewish Shema.

Mohammed mentions the Biblical names Adam, Moses, Abraham, Isaac, Jacob, Ishmael and others several times in the Quran, but these names have not been documented as existing before his time Also, there is no genealogical or other documentary proof that the Arabs descend from Ishmael. Maybe future DNA and anthropological studies will be able to throw more light on the various, pre-historic Semitic bloodlines.

As noted, Mohammed initially favored the Jews and Christians. When still in Mecca, his followers prayed in the direction (qibla) of Jerusalem. But, when he fled to Medina in 622 due to the hostility of the then unconverted Arab majority and the openly skeptical Jews and Christians, he consolidated his followers into a small army and retook Mecca. In punishment of the disloyal Jews and Christians, he changed the qibla to Mecca.

At that time he also received the violent, anti-Jewish and anti-Christian jihadic "Medina message", now the first half of the Quran. From the time of those hostile experiences stem his God-given diatribes in the Quran against all Christians and Jews, as quoted above. But remember that the shorter, peaceful verses in the back of the Quran are the ones given by Allah to the Prophet before his flight from Mecca - the Mecca message.

It bears repeating that the longer, violent passages date from his sojourn in Medina and after. The reason that these later passages are now in the first half of the Quran is that they are considered to be of overriding importance because of their emphasis on jihad against all non-Muslim religions and regimes. Also, we must not forget that the peaceful Mecca message in the back of the Quran can never be interpreted as a peaceful attitude towards non-believers. That idea has been totally superseded by the Medina jihad message. There is therefore a religious as well as a strategic reason for its having been placed in the first half of the Quran. Nowadays,

59

the peaceful Mecca message in the back applies strictly to Muslims, not to the outside non-believers.

Muslim ideology has a noticeable echo of the violence, rigidity and intolerance of communism, with this difference, that communism in the Soviet Union was an ideology enforced from the top down and therefore vulnerable in the long run, whereas Islamic violence comes from the religion of the common man and energizes the system from the bottom up. This has resulted in strong religious and political cohesion in Muslim society.

History has shown that through almost 14 centuries Islam has been on the one hand hard and monolithic and on the other hand resilient and enduring. That makes the Muslim drive for world dominance ten times as dangerous and effective as communism ever was.

Will it become the next World Empire after the United States? We shall see.

One more point needs to be cleared up, namely the folk-belief that Allah is the same God as the God of the Jews and the Christians. That is not so: all three are different. Not only do these three religions have three different names for the divinity, namely Allah, Yahoveh (pronounced as Adonai) and God, but it is very obvious that the Islamic Allah is a God of war, the Christian God is a God of love, and the Jewish God is monotheistic, with its own Revelation of a God who looks after his chosen, persecuted and suffering people and will one day send them the Messiah.

It also appears that the differences between these three religions are due to subjective interpretation of the divine will by each of the three founders, Moses, Jesus and Mohammed. Each Revelation has a personal touch.

Jesus encapsulated Moses' laws in His original message of repentance (to God) and love (of neighbor),

60

identical to His saying "Love God above all (repentance) and your neighbor as yourself. This is still an authentic Jewish belief as well.

But Paul's message was not quite the same as that of Jesus. Jesus exalted God and Paul exalted Jesus. Much later, several reformers put their own subjective stamp on the Protestant faith: Luther, Calvin, Menno Simons, Wesley and Joseph Smith.

So it is evident that all religions and denominations have their origin in a leader who, in his own mind, fashioned an unparalleled height of understanding of God, fitting into the needs of his time and whose beliefs became enshrined, respectively, in a Holy Book or in a dogmatic thesis.

How does this apply to Mohammed? Well, when he thought he could still win the Christians and Jews over to him in Mecca, his message was tolerant and peaceful. However, as soon as these two groups turned against him, the message from Allah became: kill the bastards. It was not: "Love your enemy", as said by his predecessor in Galilee, but "Kill the Jews and Christians". The words he used for them, "the vilest of animals", is quite close to the colloquial term I used.

So in the Muslim method of evangelizing the whole world by force we still see the "genius" of 622 who combined the desert way of absorbing hostile tribes through murder and rape with a revelation of divinely inspired hate of other religions—all laid down in a Holy Book that empowered successive generations to smash their way across the known world, leaving only the ruins of once flourishing Mediterranean civilizations.

During a series of lectures in Amherst, New York—the freethinkers' capital of the U.S.—a few years ago, I had the temerity to argue that the Muslim religion had a violent streak. "That's a lot of bull', snarled the libertarian next to me and the next day he thrust a long list of peaceful texts from the Quran under my nose—all from the Mecca message!

Little did he know that a few miles away, in Masten, the Sunni mullahs teach their students the whole Quran which emphasizes the Medina message.

The betrayal of the American people

This Medina message, more than any other part of the Quran, teaches the Muslim that his religion is superior to all others and that it must become universal. There is only one State that is free and true and that is the State where the religion of Islam is the supreme guide in politics, education, occupation, law, morals and all other social aspects. Every Muslim is still bound by the provisions laid down in the Quran almost 1400 years ago. The rules of war that were then valid are just as scrupulously followed today. Western democracy and the separation of church and state to a Muslim mind are godless travesties—human rebellion against the Almighty. From what we have gathered so far, one may well wonder how the teaching of "the whole Quran" affects the minds of school-age Muslim children in America. This is one of the most worrisome aspects of the presence of the 5 to 6 million Muslims in America.

Nothing illustrates this problem better than an incident in which the writer was involved several years ago in a northeastern U.S. city. The occasion was a public neighborhood meeting concerning a proposal by the Muslim community to convert a large, formerly public building, totally surrounded by thick, high, stone walls, into a Muslim center of learning, including a mosque and a school.

I suggested to the audience to be wary of such a proposal since the walls added a type of seclusion to the complex that would make it difficult for the public or the government to scrutinize whether the schoolchildren would be taught any religiously tinted anti-American themes. One of the white-robed Muslim clerics on the podium then asked me how much I knew about the Quran.

By way of answer I explained to the audience that the Quran contains two messages, one the peaceful Mecca message and the other the violent Medina one. Then I asked the mullahs if they would refrain from teaching the latter. One of them stood up, straightened himself to his full length, pushing his chest out in contempt at the question and said coldly: "WE ARE SUNNIS AND WE TEACH THE WHOLE QURAN".

At that moment I knew enough and abruptly left the meeting, but I was followed by a small crowd of reporters and the white-robed mullahs who all kept peppering me with questions. Finally, after making a short statement, I saw an opening and drove off.

An equally piquant moment befell President George W. Bush, when during his first term he attended a large gathering of a national Muslim association. When it was the President's turn to speak, he tried to win some favor (and possibly some votes) at the end of his address by expressing his fond hope that all Muslims might work hand-in-hand with their fellow-Americans for the good of all. In reply, the white-robed leader of the affair remarked, somewhat curtly; "YES, MR. PRESIDENT, THAT MIGHT BE POSSIBLE IF THE AMERICAN PEOPLE WOULD SEE THE TRUTH".

Instead of telling the cleric in front of the whole audience to apologize for that brazen affront, the President just sat there, probably stunned, and took the slap in his face. Had he stood up and put the man in his place, he might have lost some Muslim votes, but the resulting publicity would have catapulted him up to the fame and integrity of a John Kennedy.

I believe that, subconsciously, the American people feel betrayed by the constant U.S. catering to the Muslim world, whether it is by the Republicans or by the Democrats. There is no decisive stand over against our new enemy and that lack of decisiveness translates into a 50-50 percentage division between the two political blocs. There is no effective, creative leadership regarding the Middle East problems to change that percentage. The public's confidence in either party's ability to make the right decisions is low. It feels betrayed.

What the government should do is to make an open-ended request to the Muslim nations to moderate the violence and hatred in their religion and become tolerant of people who think and worship differently. But it is too timid to even draw the least bit of attention to the most critical source of friction between the Western world and Islam. Somebody in high office should take the bull by the horn, admit the weaknesses and looseness of our post-Christian civilization and ask the Muslims to do the same for Islam. Not opening such a debate is betrayal of the values Americans cherish.

Some Muslim educators are well aware of the explosive content of the Medina message in the Quran. A few moderates have suggested de-emphasizing or even "abrogating" it in view of its conflict with the growing recognition of basic human rights in an international context.

To actively promote such a goal, an Islamic reformist group called the Republican Brothers was started. However, several founding members were imprisoned and their leader, Mahmoud Mohammed Taha, was executed in Khartoum, Sudan, in 1985 by order of the President, Gaafar Mohammed al-Numeiry, for apostasy and defaming the Quran.

In his now famous tract "The Second Message of Islam", Taha had argued that, although Muslim opposition to Western neocolonialism and cultural domination was justified, the imposition of Islamic holy law (the Sharia) was no longer acceptable in light of the ORIGINAL Mecca Message.

In 2002, Professor An-Naim, formerly of the Sudan, elaborated on Taha's ideas. He regretted that the Islamic world had never experienced the equivalent of the European Enlightenment and the Reformation which had led to a system of representative government first and subsequently to human rights, civil liberties, technology and new inventions. He lauded countries like Turkey and Egypt that had successfully integrated the better aspects of Western human progress with some of the requirements of sharia, avoiding western abuses with regard to sex, materialism and immodesty.

No doubt influenced by the recent 9/11 event, he pointed out that the time had come to take the further step of ABROGATING THE MEDINA MESSAGE because of its extreme emphasis on killing Jews and Christians as unbelievers. Since Sharia law endorses extending Muslim rule through the killing of infidels wherever they are found, he proposed that it be replaced by reform laws based on the earlier MECCA founding message.

If such an incisive reform of Islam could ever be made, it would obviously eliminate much of the need for American policing of the Middle East The clash of civilizations, so convincingly argued by Huntington and now in its beginning stages in Iraq and elsewhere in the Middle East, could also be avoided.

But is it realistic? It is almost like asking Christianity to abrogate St. Paul's message about Jesus and just keep

Jesus' message about the Kingdom of God. What would be left of the Latter Day Saints if they were asked to drop the book of Mormon? It is just impossible for any self-respecting religious movement to prune away such a large part of its Revealed Truth.

The only possible way to affect Islam would be for some zealous Christians to fiercely start learning Arabic and inundate the Middle East with an easy to understand Christian message, not denouncing Muslim morals, but deploring our own as well. Terms such as repentance, salvation, and eternal life could be replaced by turn-around, rescue, and New Life. Don't preach, but gently ask. Address them as "we", never "you". Maybe make some trial runs with the American Muslims first and learn. That is building up America, not betraying it.

Can Muslims be loyal citizens?

And this brings us smack back to the U.S., where some five million Muslims of Middle Eastern origin are taught to believe in THE WHOLE QURAN.

How can this group, which is told to kill unbelievers, be truly and undividedly loyal to America? All world religions except Islam advocate love and peace. Islam is totally intolerant of all other religions and demands that they be destroyed. In other words, a Muslim's first loyalty is not to an America as it exists, but to a future America changed into an Islamic entity through jihad. A Muslim's oath of loyalty is just perjury.

This problem must be met head-on and discussed freely and openly, not pushed under the table as the government does. The following true incident will demonstrate the psychological pressure that clerics will use to make any believer obey them.

When Muslim fanatics were ambushing and terrorizing the Kosovo Serbs in the late 1990s in order to claim Kosovo for Islam, a cleric told a Muslim villager that he must kill his Serbian Orthodox neighbor. Vehemently protesting, he told the cleric he would never do that; his neighbor had been his friend ever since he grew up; they had helped each other, went places together and visited each other often. The cleric smiled and left.

The next evening he came back with the Quran, explaining to the man that Allah wanted him to slay his neighbors; that not he himself but Allah would actually do the slaying and that it would be a good deed for the glory of Islam. If he obeyed, he would be rewarded with Heaven. After some more misgivings and pleadings by the villager, he was told he would go to the eternal fires of Hell, if he did not obey Allah. This is the penalty that every Muslim dreads the most, more than death itself.

The cleric left and that night the villager killed his neighbor, the neighbor's wife and their children. Because he lived so nearby and had always been good friends with his neighbor, the man was never suspected. But in literal fulfillment of the Quran, the act struck terror into the hearts of the Serbian villagers and many left for safer places.

The Muslim marauders stuck another victory feather in their hats and were off to other parts to continue their holy deeds against Serbian Kosovo. They almost lost the battle to a wily Milosevich, but fortunately Bill Clinton helped them with his bombers, to the greater glory of Allah.

Will American Muslims be persuaded like the villager, if they are told by their clerics on some future day what to do against America? THEY WILL. Why does the

U.S. government not concentrate primarily on the Muslim challenge in the U.S. instead of betraying the American public through the wholesale imposition of new security laws on the entire population?

Only the Muslim sector of the population, the one that is ideologically bound to kill all Christians and Jews, should be subject to surveillance, because its religious tenets run totally contrary to the Constitution and human rights. Nobody else in America is allowed to openly or secretly belong to a sect or group whose aim is the violent overthrow of the government for religious reasons. Yet the U.S. makes an exception for the Muslims. When letting these immigrants into the country, the U.S. should have known that they were allowing the proverbial camel to stick his head into the tent.

That shortsighted, ill-focused immigration policy was the first part of the next betrayal. The second part was to misinform the American public, claiming that 9/11 was done by some Muslim bandits who hated America. Why not honestly admit that these Muslims did this out of their misguided conviction that they were doing it for the glory of God?

Both the immigration policy and the misinformation were telltale signs of American catering to the tender feelings of the cruel Islamic world. The third part of this particular betrayal was the deference to Islam in applying the new anti-terrorist security measures in such a way that they would not only diminish the civil rights of the Muslim minority, but of the entire population. All Americans must suffer so that America can never be accused of even the slightest affront to Islam.

To stop this ugly nonsense, the U.S. should call a spade a spade, just like they did when exposing the virulence of Naziism and Communism. It should require all Muslims in the U.S. over the age of sixteen to repudiate and forswear orally and in writing all the texts in the Quran that compel them to mistreat or kill Jews, Christians or members of any other religion on pain of exile. Each Muslim, immigrant or born here, should add his or her fingerprints and photo to such declaration. The document should at all times be carried on the person when at large.

Please note these requirements should not in any way prohibit the bearer from freedom of worship, movement or association. In fact, the document would increase the Muslim's freedoms, because only those who make the declaration would be left in the country. Those who refused would lose their citizenship and right to be in the United States. This would not be discrimination against a minority, but an anti-terrorist measure against persons who by definition hold beliefs dangerous to the security of the United States and in violation of the Constitution. Those who volunteer to forswear the jihad verses should be given A-one citizen status.

This action would also help remove American antipathy against Muslims, because those who signed off on jihad could now be fully trusted, leading to new bonds of friendship. All Muslim visitors from abroad, especially from nearby Canada and Mexico, should be required to take the oath as well. Should there be any outbreak of Muslim violence against other citizens, partial or local martial law should be declared and offenders summarily exiled after a military tribunal hearing.

Americans must no longer tolerate the intrusion on their privacy, movement and communications because of what a few did. The security acts should be abridged or abolished and the police stopped from detaining anyone without first giving a valid reason. As it is, the anti-terrorist laws tend to function as a dragnet for catching people who have nothing to do with terrorism. The American people should not continue to be pushed, shoved, restricted, harassed and punished for the acts of those 19 Muslim terrorists that panicked the American leaders on September 11, 2001.

Instead, Americans should insist that the government do its utmost to ensure that the ANTI-AMERICAN BIAS, promoted by the aforementioned jihad verses is no longer taught in Muslim schools, mosques or other gatherings. This should help the U.S. get rid of the arrogant, fanatical clerics we met on previous pages. This would be no more discriminatory than the prosecution of the Mafia, Neo-Nazis, white supremacists or violent anarchists.

Unfortunately there exists a governmental roadblock against the suggestions just put forward. The government never acts, unless the people get hurt first.

The Islamic train rumbles on

Although we can see that the fatwa by bin Laden gave new impetus to Muslim jihad, anti-Westernism actually has a longer history. It did not start with 9/11 or the 1983 attack on the American-French Headquarters in Beirut. In recent history it was first witnessed in its ugliest form in the Turkish genocide of the Christian Armenians in 1915-1916. It can also be traced to the initial defeat of the colonial powers in the Far East by the Japanese in World War II. For instance, the Japanese showed the Indonesians and other European colonies that the West was not invincible and falsely told them that after the war was won by Japan, each nation would become independent under Japanese protection. As we saw before, the U.S. encouraged the drive for independence through its shortsighted anti-colonial policy and unrealistic dreams of democracy for these new nations. After British India and the Dutch East Indies, the colonies, many of them Muslim, fell like dominos. The Muslims saw the rapid capitulation by the colonial powers as a sign of weakness.

Significantly, the 1989 end of the Soviet occupation of Afghanistan that came about largely through massive American intervention was subsequently celebrated as a victory for the Afghans only. The truth is that this war could never have been won by either the Americans or the Afghans alone. However, we also know now that the strength of small groups of Muslim militants, sheltered by the civilian population, cannot be underrated. As proved in Kosovo, the insurgents can operate in any Muslim country and, through constant unrest and terror methods, find weak spots in Western strategy and diplomacy that can be exploited for the glory of Allah.

The 1983 American pull-out from Lebanon after the terrorist bombing that killed 242 Americans, the 1993 U.S. withdrawal from Somalia after the dragging of an American soldier's body through Mogadishu, the successful attack on the USS Cole in the port of Aden in 2000 are all seen by the TV watching Muslims as signs of a weak America and a powerful Allah. Modern terrorism has a long genealogy of murderous men.

The lesson in all this is that the U.S. should never again attempt costly, fruitless, positional warfare with front lines, tanks, encampments and surface logistics against Muslim insurgents. But the High Command is slow to learn. The main U.S. strength lies in its present ability to wage sophisticated, high-technology wars from the air with pinpoint accuracy of observing and hitting from great heights. On the ground, it would be more effective to use the divide and rule tricks.

Before we go on, let us take a last look at 9/11, this time from a purely religious Muslim viewpoint. It has been detected that the original plan of attack was five jihadists to each plane, but one was detained before he could board. This would have made a total of twenty. And what does the Quran say in Sura 8:65?

IF THERE ARE TWENTY PATIENT (CALM) ONES AMONGST YOU, THEY WILL OVERCOME TWO HUNDRED.

There can only be one explanation for this "coincidence", namely that it wasn't coincidence at all, but in planned response to the Quran. That the number of two hundred was surpassed, by far, bin Laden must have attributed to Allah.

According to the Quran, these men incurred no moral guilt, but were simply the tools in Allah's hands and would be rewarded with immediate admission to Paradise. Although suicide in the general sense is forbidden, a suicidal death on behalf of jihad is considered to be a martyr's self-sacrifice "in the way of Allah".

Masoumen Ebketar, a high-ranking moderate woman member of the Mohamed Khatami government in Iran, posited that Islam is basically a politically oriented religion. Comparing this fact with the struggle between Khatami as a modernizer and the Ayatollah of Iran as a devoted Islamist (and the strongest leader in Iran) we must conclude that, in the case of Iran,

    a)   a separation of mosque and state is impossible;
    b)   a secular government is as yet improbable;
    c)   the "whole Quran" prevents reform of Islam;
    d)   it is impossible to inject democracy into a system where politics is totally defined by religion;

e) but a U.S. offer of a greater Shia bloc might induce the Ayatollah to make crucial political concessions.

In England, it took over 600 years to progress from absolute monarchy since Magna Carta, (1215 A.D.) to representative government in 1832 (Reform bill); in the rest of Europe it did not take hold until about 1848.

What took the Western world six hundred years and cost millions of lives through revolutions, schisms and civil wars cannot be duplicated in a few decades by a Middle East civilization that has been marked by the same politico-religious system for almost one thousand and four hundred years.

Ingrained in the minds of countless generations of Muslims is the conviction that there can be no universal peace or freedom until the earth is entirely subjected to Islam. To a Muslim, the world is divided into two camps: the world of peace (Dar al-Islam) and the world of war (Dar al-Harb). Where, either through expansion of the Muslim population (as in Kosovo, Kashmir, the Sudan and Lebanon) or through aggression from the outside (by the U.S., for example), the world of Islam must be safeguarded, it is the duty of each Muslim to defend Islam by taking up arms (al-harb) against the infidel.

This also precludes peace between the Muslim world and Israel since Israel is considered to be occupying Muslim land. This means that eventually all Israelis must be either removed or killed. It also means that Israel must never give in to any Muslim demands whatsoever, because it will never be enough. As soon as it lets down any of its defenses, it will be lost. The time may well come when Israel will have to do some removing of Muslims. Whatever happens, Israel is condemned to eternal war.

The colonization of Indonesia by the Netherlands from the 1600s to the mid 1900s made only small Christian inroads into the indigenous Muslim population, mainly in Timor, the Moluckas and the island of Tulawesi. After independence all these Christians experienced Muslim repression and many fled.

Likewise, Egypt, Syria and Iraq, largely Christian nations until the seventh century, were quickly Islamized through tremendous slaughter during and after the Muslim invasions of 637 and 640. Only small pockets of Christians still survive there and even fewer Jews. Remarkably, the original language of Egypt, Coptic, is now only preserved in the Christian Coptic Church. Arabic was forced on the converted majority.

The Crusades, from 1096 to 1300, did little to establish a permanent Christian presence in what was left of the Holy Land. Rivalry between the Roman Catholic and Greek Orthodox leaders resulted in the sacking of Byzantium by the Roman Catholics during the Fourth Crusade in 1204, considerably weakening both the city walls and the Orthodox Empire.

Had the Roman ecclesiastical leaders looked farther ahead, putting aside their dogmatic gripes, a united stand against the Muslims would have prevented the eventual conquest of an inadequately walled city in 1453. That loss in turn laid the Balkans open to further Muslim slaughter and conquest, severely threatening the interests of the Roman Catholic Church itself.

Although Spain was freed from the last remaining Muslim ruler in 1492 under King Ferdinand and Queen Isabella, the Orthodox Balkans, once again unaided by their fellow Christians, were overrun by the murderous Muslim hordes. Untold multitudes of Christian Serbs and Croats were massacred, raped, enslaved and islamized.

Twice, Turkish armies stood before the gates of Vienna. One of my direct ancestors, Jakob Dunwald (9 generations back) had a brother who, in 1683 as General Dunwald in the Brandenburg army, together with his brother-in-law, General Ernst Rudiger von Starhemberg and their troops, held the besieged, starving city against all odds until the arrival of the relieving Allied armies. The Allies then decimated the Turks.

Today's lack of cohesion between the U.S. and Europe in the face of the common Muslim danger has an ominous parallel with the friction between the Catholic and Orthodox factions of Christianity many centuries ago. Those who are ignorant of their history are doomed to repeat it.

Like the Communist threat and its Fifth Column during the Cold War, the intolerant Muslim religion and its terrorist vanguard are now the gravest threat to European democracy and civilization. President Bush once described the Muslim terrorists as having hijacked a "noble" religion, but that was a disingenuous use of diplomat-speak, designed to distance the Islamists from mainline Islam, which is like trying to separate the "good" murderers from the "bad" ones.

Although the U.S. needs Middle Eastern oil, there is nothing so troubling as to see the U.S. letting Muslim nations profit by making nuclear weapons. The 9/11 event should have given the U.S. enough cause to destroy the nuclear potential of both Pakistan and Iran (an alternative to a nuclear bomb on bin Laden?) in a couple of raids. The Muslim world would have sat up and taken notice: "Do these guys mean business?" The last thing the U.S. needs is an Islamist nuclear threat to the West.

As suggested above, there is a relatively straightforward way of solving the Iraq crisis. It is ten times better for the

U.S. .to throw its weight behind the Shias than letting Iran take the lead. The U.S. must roll with the punches. It should have learned by now that continued slaughter of Al-Sadr's followers to appease the Sunnis is not only suicidal, but playing into the hands of the Sunnis.

It is quite clear from Al-Sadr's cease-fire tactics that he wants the U.S. to understand that he needs to fight the Sunnis, not U.S. troops. But the U.S. is deaf. So he simply keeps waiting until the U.S. withdraws.

Looking at the Middle East problems in the long view the U.S. struggle in Iraq is unique; it is really the war against Sunni terrorism guided by a Sunni bin-Laden. It is in America's long-term advantage to give the Shias breathing room in Iraq. The U.S. can head off Iran by usurping its role as helper of Shia Iraq. The war would end. The Sunni insurgency would be stopped by Iraq's new Shia army and the strained relations with Iran patched up.

If bin Laden continues his jihad against the U.S. and remains resolved to Islamize the West, then the U.S. will be left with no other choice (after Naziism and Communism) but to identify the religious malevolence inherent in Islam as the last remaining international ideological threat to Western freedom to be destroyed.

This plan should be begun now, not through war, but through a tricky policy similar to Reagan's Star Wars project, which brought the mighty Soviet Union to its knees. If the U.S. waits any longer, continuing its naive policy of Muslim appeasement, like Chamberlain and Daladier tried on Hitler, it will soon be too late and it will cause a Third World War. That war must be avoided at all costs because of its gruesomeness

Twenty years from now, the centers of world power will have shifted; the U.S. may no longer be in a position to use its awesome power at will, because China and Russia will have matured to play major roles in world politics. Now is the time.

Alas, alas, the signs are that the West will continue to be soft on Islam. The unpleasant consequences of that shortsighted policy will draw Europe and America into an ever faster moving vortex of Islamic infiltration and expansion that no amount of new strategies will allow the U.S. to escape.

Al Qaida, Islam's Fifth Column, is patiently looking for new weaknesses in the U.S. systems to deliver another blow.

Chances are bin Laden will acquire a nuclear weapon, deliver it to the U.S. by stealth, (possibly even by air) and flatten a large city. If that caused one million casualties and the U.S. retaliated tenfold—it would still hurt the U.S. more because of its highly sensitive, integrated and interdependent industrial-commercial complex. Retaliation would have to be a massive hundredfold to even the score—an unimaginable act of war.

What are the costs of the present U.S. policy of waging conventional, situation warfare instead of divide and rule? The enormous monetary strain on the economy of conducting endless campaigns against suicidal Islamic terrorism in more and more parts of the world is bound to reach a point beyond which we can only see serious damage to the U.S. economy and its status as superpower. On the other hand, jihad warfare costs only a fraction of what the U.S. has to spend, so in the end it will be a losing game, not only for America, but for the entire Western world. We already saw this unbalance in the costs of 9/11.

People of America: rest assured that by trying to democratize the Muslim world and making it a third world industrial and political powerhouse without humanizing Muslim militant beliefs or doing something about its enormous population growth, you are digging your own grave

You will simply be overwhelmed by Islam within a hundred years, fully in accord with valid projections of Muslim population growth.

5.   THE WORLD AGAINST THE JEWS

The long road of suffering and rejection

The successive calamities that have struck the Hebrew people throughout history are almost unparalleled in the documents of human suffering and persecution.

Deported, beaten, forcibly converted, beheaded and gassed, only a fraction of their potential numbers survives, yet continuing an unbroken legacy of some 6,000 years. A large part of the globe indirectly owes its monotheism to the Jews.

The reason for their indomitable will to overcome all adversities, no matter how abject, can be ascribed to the fact that they were among the first nations led by gifted leaders whose revelations were put together in a Holy Book. This moral guide sustained them through the ages, giving them literacy, faith and social cohesion from generation to generation.

As noted before, the Hebrew tongue is a Semitic dialect, distantly related to Phoenician, Arabic, Aramaic and other Middle Eastern languages. To what extent the people speaking these different languages are ethnically related to each other, the waiting is for more advanced DNA research. If our Western technology-driven civilization endures for another hundred years, we can expect the most astonishing refinements and breakthroughs in the study of anthropology, archaeology and linguistics. The results will hopefully also throw more light on the centuries of mixing and moving of prehistoric tribes. Maybe some day we will have electronic gadgets that can "read" the stratified surfaces that make up the earth's crust.

The best, but often rare guides to historic reconstruction are fragments of old writing such as the Egyptian hieroglyphics, Hittite inscriptions and the Dead Sea Scrolls, the latter seeming to date from the era just before the destruction of the Hebrew Temple in the year 70.

The first destruction of the Jewish temple in Jerusalem took place around the year 586 B.C., followed by the forced transplantation of thousands of Jewish families to Babylon. According to the book of Ezra, a sizable number were allowed to return to Jerusalem in later years. There they renewed the worship of the One God and the observance of the Law, contained in the Torah, which means Instruction (in the Truth).

The second destruction of the temple in 70 saw the banishment of practically all Jewry from Jerusalem and Judea. Again, a remnant returned and there are even places in the north of present-day Israel, such as Safed and Pekin where some Jewish families have lived uninterruptedly for the past two thousand years or more. A tempting area for a DNA project! No doubt some survived in the environs of Jerusalem as well.

The Holy Roman Empire which lasted roughly from the time of Charlemagne in the 800s to the Reformation in the late 1500s was a semi-theocracy somewhat like the conglomeration of Middle Eastern, Turkish and North African countries that are bound together by Islam.

The early Roman Catholic Church saw itself as the only true religious authority on earth. Wary of heresy, it was very intolerant of Jews and Muslims and as tough on Greek Orthodox Christians as Muslims are on the U.S. today. From scanty memoirs of the Middle Ages we get the earliest documentation of the persecution of Jews in Europe by Catholicism.

In what could be termed the first Holocaust, practically all the Jews in Jerusalem were burned alive in their numerous synagogues in 1099, when the entire city was put to the torch by the regiments of Catholic Europe's chivalry during the First Crusade, which started in 1095. On their way to the Holy Land, while still in Europe, the Catholic barons also wanted to show their zeal for Catholicism by looting and annihilating Jewish ghettoes in Worms, Mainz, Cologne and other places.

The hot hatred and cruelty against the so-called "Christ-killing Jews", the indifference to the horrible screams of the women and children and the religious satisfaction of "doing a good work" were absolutely no different from the merciless methods used by Mohammed and his followers that we reviewed earlier. They have thrown an indelible moral stain on the Church of those days, a stain of barbarity only lately acknowledged and condemned by Pope John Paul II in an official declaration and request for forgiveness.

But Catholicism had already been hard on the Jews since shortly after it had become the official religion of the Roman Empire in 313. Saint Augustine (354-430), formulated the harsh doctrine that since Catholicism was now the only religion, people should no longer have the choice of belonging or not. The Church would define heresy, while the State (now also Catholic) would punish it. He laid down the basis of an intolerant religious theocracy that would lead to the Inquisition, bringing death to tens of thousands of Jews and heretics, a "routine" that went on unchecked until the Reformation.

As early as 576 the Jewish settlement near Lyons, France, was given the choice of either becoming Catholic or being exiled.

In 637, five years after the death of Mohammed, it was the Muslims who, when conquering Jerusalem, cleared the land of both Jews and Christians. Both had to flee before the conquering Muslim bands, when almost the entire Mediterranean region was Islamized through death, rape, looting and enslavement. Only remnants survived in Syria and Egypt.

The bitter irony in all this was that, while Catholics could find refuge in other Catholic lands, the Jews had nowhere to go. There was no other Jewish country. So they became skilled at paying off certain Catholic princes, nobles or even bishops for protection in their fortresses in times of acute danger. They found they could do the same thing in Muslim areas, after asking for asylum there from Catholic persecution. For several hundred years the Jews enjoyed a certain amount of freedom in Muslim Spain.

At times, laws were enacted forcing Jews to wear badges or distinctive clothing. And they were often accused of the ritual use of Christian blood, an undeserved stigma called blood libel. It was based on rumor, superstition, jealousy, lies and plain hatred. But the resulting killings, whether by the sword, hanging or drowning were often extensive, fanned by the prejudices of the uneducated rabble, although opposed in name by the bishops and magistrates who preferred court proceedings.

During the reign of the Russian Orthodox czars, Jews were often mercilessly exploited and persecuted. Many died in massacres in Poland as well.

In 1492, Catholic Spain expelled all Jews, many of them skilled tradesmen and artisans that had long been an economic attribute to the country. Some resettled in Protestant capitals such as Berlin and Amsterdam where they contributed to commercial life and general economic progress.

But many Protestant princes, as well as the public, treated Jews as second-class citizens through all kinds of discrimination. Antipathy to the Jews lurked in England and later in the U.S.

The greatest crime against the Jews in all history occurred during World War II in Nazi-occupied countries where six million died in the Holocaust, the most heinous, unprecedented plan to exterminate European Jewry.

In the occupied countries, even in Germany itself, many people risked their lives hiding Jews in lofts, hidden rooms, barns or shelters dug in the ground.

Yet it is amazing how widespread was the low esteem of Jews before and during World War II in the West, including the U.S.

In 1939, Cuba refused entry to 637 Jews on board the steamer "St. Louis" that had left Hamburg, Germany, on May 13, still almost three years before the "final solution". When the captain, Gustav Schroeder, together with the Jewish leaders on board, tried other Caribbean countries, they met nothing but obstacles. But what is significant is that even the United States rebuffed the Jews – a vast difference from today, when Latino, Asiatic and African "refugees" enter in droves.

When finally there was no other choice for the captain but to return to Europe, four countries, Belgium, France, The Netherlands and England each took in about a quarter of the refugees. Those that went to England, were the luckiest, for the other countries were subsequently overrun by the Germans and about half of the returnees were caught and died in the notorious extermination camps.

Reportedly, another ship load of German fugitive Jews was also turned back to Germany. On arrival, they were vilified, spat upon and pelted with stones by selected Nazis on disembarking and sent to the concentration camps to die.

The Zionist movement, designed to find a place for the luckless wandering Jews, met fierce resistance by the British, when boatloads of Jewish emigres from all over Europe tried to enter Palestine by stealth. The Brits, responsible for peace in Palestine under a post-World War I mandate, had adopted a policy of appeasing the anti-Jewish Muslims by setting low entry quotas for Jewish refugees wishing to go to Palestine. A cat and mouse game developed, with the Jews sneaking through the blockade of ships guarding the coast and the British catching and interning many of the illegal boatloads. The situation was extremely ticklish between 1945 and 1948—that is, until the establishment of the Israeli nation.

One such attempt by the Jews recently received the spotlight when Yossi Harel, the captain of one of those people-smuggling boats, died in Tel Aviv on Saturday, April 26, 2008, aged 90. In the summer of 1947, he tried to steer his ship, known as the "Exodus 47", carrying 4,500 Holocaust survivors, through a line of British ships but was caught. A fight apparently ensued between the desperate emigres and the British agents who boarded the ship, resulting in the deaths of three people.

In red-hot anger, the British sent the ship back to Europe where it became a symbol of the plight of the landless Jews. After receiving widespread publicity and sympathy, the event helped the Jewish cause for a homeland in Palestine.

A similar event, but with a much more tragic ending, is told in the gripping story by Douglas Frantz and Catherine Collins of the barge "Struma", which exploded mysteriously on the Black Sea February 24, 1942 with an estimated 781 Jewish refugees and a crew of ten. Only one passenger, David Stoliar, survived.

After hair-raising escapes from the watchful eyes of the police, walking by night, riding on rickety farm carts, coming from all over Romania, the Jews arrived in Bucharest, its capital. There they were locked in a sealed train, arriving at the port of Constantia on December 7, 1941, to eventually board the "Struma", a large, former cattle ship—with a defective engine – hastily made over for human transport.

Leaving port December 12, the ship had several engine failures, resulting in it being towed to Istanbul December 15.

Desperate efforts were made to enlist Turkish and British help towards possible transportation to Cyprus, but they all ended up in fruitless dialogue between a Turkish government unwilling to help Jews and a British government scared to inflame Muslim tempers in Palestine. Was the engine deliberately made unworkable to get a Turkish or other ship to take the refugees anywhere except back to Europe?

After endless haggling and stalling, the Turkish government made the cruel decision to tow the Struma with its tired, cold, emaciated, helpless and hopeless passengers out of port and back onto the Black Sea, where the ropes were cut and the Struma set adrift. The date was February 23, 1942. The next day a torpedo of oft-debated origin tore a huge hole in the ship, which started to sink immediately. Most of the passengers drowned at the time of impact, several floated or swam for a few minutes in the ice-cold water, screaming and praying in the face of certain death, while others held on longer to pieces of wood. However, the freezing winter cold overcame them all in the end,

Only one determined survivor clinging to a large deck piece found the superhuman strength of will and endurance to make it through the night. Half-frozen and barely able to move, he was spotted the next day by a passing ship that signaled a boathouse. He was then rowed ashore by the Turkish workers.

The Turkish government did all it could to smother the existence of the survivor, but through a stroke of luck, a Swiss reporter spoke to Stoliar in French while the latter was being escorted to the hospital. Stoliar understood and in halting words gave his name and the fact that he was a survivor of the Struma sinking. The reporter cabled the news to Reuters immediately.

Without that chance encounter the world might never have known about Stoliar. He was lodged in prison for being in Turkey illegally, that is, without a visa, and he might very well have rotted there, or in some other way forever silenced. That way, the Turkish government would never be suspected of deliberately abandoning the Jews on an unseaworthy ship on a dangerous stretch of the Black Sea.

Eventually, through international efforts, helped by the media publicity, he was set free almost two months later and, after a stint in the British army, made it to Israel.

The broader circumstances under which the Struma met its mortal fate can once again be seen in the by now familiar light of the West fearing to help the Jews in case that should ruffle Muslim feathers, even when it saw the utmost brutal Muslim disregard for the infidel's life, especially Jewish life.

A diving expedition in the year 2000 to locate the remains of the Struma, led by Michael Buxton (changed from Bucspan), whose parents had been passengers on the Struma, produced inconclusive results. Perhaps new attempts could be made with more sophisticated cameras and scanning instruments, or even with a small submarine, using the Soviet coordinates given at the time of the sinking.

The name Langenmass in the back of the Frantz/Collins book on the Struma is interesting, because it is very close to Langnas, a 1939 passenger on the St. Louis mentioned in the "Voyage of the Damned" by Thomas and Witts.

Inasmuch as the Holocaust can never receive enough attention, I will mention one more episode, itself a full picture of the cruelty of the Nazi death camps, in which the Jewish inmates struck an extraordinary deal with the camp commander. It was based on the time-honored, holy wish of each Jewish father to perpetuate his line for the Lord through one or more sons.

They offered to sacrifice themselves by all going voluntarily to the gas chambers with their wives if their children would be spared.

Elsewhere we learn of an entire field full of thinly-clad, hungry, shivering, crying Jewish children who were left to their own devices in the middle of winter, while the S. S. camp commander dickered with other authorities whether the deal could be honored or not. I do not know the final outcome.

A surviving spectator described the youngsters' keening as a surreal cacophony of endless, heartrending sobbing and moaning, rising and falling like waves, the desperate little faces showing the incomprehension of being abandoned by their parents and no one to turn to for protection.

Is the wandering Jew gone?

A political and moral dilemma of global proportions arose when the greatly diminished Jews of the world took their destiny into their own hands by re-conquering their ancient homeland from the Muslim Palestinians. But it has become an insoluble problem because the Palestinians, like

87

all other Muslims, adhere to the ancient Quranic instruction to "drive the unbelievers out from where they drove you out" (Sura 2:191).

This intransigence comes into sharp focus in the way freedom of religion works in the West as compared to the Muslim East. In the U.S., Muslims can build mosques, freely practice their religion and even win converts. In a Muslim country, a Christian or a Jew must keep a very low profile. They can practice their religion, but almost nowhere are they allowed to build new churches or synagogues and they cannot convert any Muslim on pain of death. There is absolutely no value balance with the West. In many ways, the Muslim theocracy is in the same position as the medieval Roman Catholic Church was when it controlled, regulated, and punished all religious thought and behavior in the Middle Ages.

The Roman Catholic Church changed, but, as we have seen on previous pages, the Muslims have a long road ahead of them towards freedom of thought, association and lifestyle.

While the Torah and the Gospels did not stop gradual advances in religious thought and critical research; with many Jews and Christians no longer taking everything in the Bible literally, the Quran works in exactly the opposite direction.

All the hostility in the Quran against Jews and Christians will forever remain the same because the Prophet said so and he is considered to have received instructions from Allah that supersede any and all pronouncements by Moses and Jesus, to say nothing of Buddha, Zoroaster or Confucius. Moreover, Muslims believe in the use of physical force to spread their superior beliefs and kill unbelievers who resist.

It is true that in early Israelite times the Hebrews were told to kill neighboring tribes that practiced idolatry and ritual child sacrifice, while likewise in the 1500s the Catholic Church massacred Incas that were given to the same orgies. It even attempted to exterminate Protestantism in the 1500s and 1600s, but Judaism and Christianity have long since mended their ways by becoming more tolerant and moderate. Jews do not proselytize and Christian missionaries use only peaceful means to make converts.

Although we cannot go deeply into religious backgrounds, mention should be made of the different methods used by Jews and Christians to resist persecution and, secondly, why Judaism became a constantly beleaguered minority, while Christianity grew to worldwide dimensions.

First off, the rebellions by the puny Jewish minority against the mighty Roman Empire were not well thought out and only led to catastrophe in the year 70, scattering the Jews in even smaller units across Asia and Europe, retaining only their religious and ethnic identity, not a national one. Their exclusive religious orientation made them social outsiders, subject to discrimination and persecution. All through the Middle Ages they fell by the hundreds and sometimes by the thousands.

For this reason they adopted a pacifist, submissive and even fatalistic attitude toward the hostile world outside, in the full conviction that the Messiah could come at any time to rescue them. It has been said that this belief was even held by some until the last moment before the gas chamber took their lives.

For hundreds of years, the Jewish prayer after meals ended with the pious plea: *"And rebuild Jerusalem, the holy city (Ubneh Yerushalaim, ir ha Kodesh), speedily and in our days; blessed art Thou o Lord, Who in His mercy will rebuild Jerusalem, Amen".* All prayer, all hope no human action.

A few exceptions to meek surrender were the heroic defense of the Warsaw ghetto against the S. S. in 1944 and the desperate, but short-lived take-over of a concentration camp.

The strength of the Catholic expansion all over the world came from constant missionary activity, starting with Jesus' disciples and, after 313, through organized church mission and papal support of Catholic regimes, first in the Frankish nation and then in the so-called Holy Roman Empire.

But its inner strength came from the ground up, because it was the belief of the common man that the Gospel should be spread. So there you have it: a universal personal faith, fervent proselytizing plus ecclesiastic and political support in national, defensible settings. It was a gigantic steamroller.

Though in its struggles with Islam, Catholicism lost the Middle East and North Africa, as well as large swaths of territory in the Balkans and Spain—it gained North and South America and recovered all of Spain and most of the Balkans.

But Kosovo was lost to Islam recently, thanks to Clinton.

Is future Israeli survival possible?

It is impossible for Israel to ever duplicate the European Christian (now Post-Christian so-called) expansion or even come close to the size of England, France or Germany. To put it closer to home, it can never equal Iran or Afghanistan. On the map, it is just a sliver of land on the East coast of the Mediterranean Sea. Is it necessary for its survival to be larger? It is an everlasting shame that Israel had to trade the Sinai for "peace", but it's a done thing.

Did the pioneers of 1948 realize that Israel would be hard put to maintain its independence as a small nation in a cauldron of Muslim hate? At least the Jews finally got the smarts to become a defensible national unit again. The slogan "never again" was the message to the world that there would never be a time again when Jews would be slaughtered in a Holocaust.

Did they finally realize that God does not rebuild Jerusalem, but that they have to do it with their own hands? That God is unable to stop Holocausts, unless the free world intervenes? One could say that the defeat of Hitler by the Allies was a roundabout measure by God to stop him. Yes, very roundabout. The proclamation of the Jewish State in 1948 was not issued by Yahveh, but by the United Nations. On the other hand it does not hurt a bit to pray and give God the glory.

But the way I sometimes pray for all kinds of foolish favors reminds me later on of the way the heathens used to pray to their idols for the same things.

The popes quickly learned that, in addition to prayer, their theocracy needed to be underpinned by earthly weapons to protect Christians. Finally, it was not the Church that halted the Muslims at Vienna's gates in 1683, but the weapons of self-interested princes. "Ora et labora" beame "Ora et pugna".

Right now, there is a serious Muslim problem lurking in the U.S., Europe and Africa. All three have a fast growing Muslim population that could be called into action by the clerics in fifty years. The six million living in the U.S. would be a much bigger voting bloc by then, enough to demand Sharia law.

Actually, Israel is already in a scenario that it will take the U.S. another 40 - 50 years to reach. The Muslims of Gaza are factually at war with Israel and the West Bank's burgeoning population will exceed Israel's in the near future. It will have its own army as well and if Israel keeps resisting U.N. and Muslim demands for a peace settlement (with all strings attached), the West Bank will start acting like Gaza.

On top of that come the threats from Iran, Lebanon and Syria, plus pressure from the U.S., pressure from Saudi Arabia and pressure from Russia. The long-term picture does not look good for Israel. What if the U.S. loses the war in Iraq? Under "losing" many military experts count a withdrawal of any kind as such. The consequences for Israel might be disastrous.

If, on the other hand, the U.S. decided to cooperate with the Shias against the Sunnis as suggested above, it could win the war in Iraq by default—freeing its hands to continue protection of Israel, to neutralize North Korea's nuclear arms threat and stop the genocide in Darfur, to mention but a few of the most desirable consequences of creative change.

Sometime in the near future, Israel may look back with nostalgia on the breather it had during the Bush administration. It is very distressing to see the U.S. so beholden to the oil sheikhs that it forever has to talk to Israel out of two opposite sides of its mouth.

As long as the Middle East has the U.S. over its slimy barrel, America's thirst for oil is its political Achilles heel. In the long run that weakness will not do Israel any good.

If the U.S. ever had to quit Iraq prematurely, either through home dissent or incessant insurgent pressure, the self-confidence of the Muslim nations would rise by leaps and bounds, possibly focusing on Israel as its next target.

The Palestinian Hamas movement is just biding its time for a U.S. withdrawal, relying on the time-proven Quranic adage of exercising patience until the time is ripe. Even Israel's atomic arsenal would be useless against thousands of jubilant, fanatic, suicidal hordes of jihadists crossing the Israeli border on foot like the Chinese crossed the Yalu en masse into North Korea.

All of Israel would be devoured by the human waves as by a locust plague and the U.S. would be confronted with the prospect of ever wider conflicts affecting its security and possibly causing a third World War. As suggested before, Iraq is crucial. The U.S. has its dagger in the heart of jihadism. It only needs a twist, a pact with the Shia opponents and the worst of the Islamic onslaught is avoidable.

If and when another oil crisis comes along and the U.S. cannot deal with the Middle East from a position of political and military strength, Israel may be forced to make degrading concessions to Hamas and Abbas.

Suppose Israel refused to make "peace" after the usual, unrealistic Palestinian charges and demands? It would have to become very "creative" to avoid the consequences of humiliating terms. Even then there would never be real peace, because whenever the Muslims see a winning streak they always want more. There can be no doubt that Israel faces eternal war.

Hence it is of no use for Israel to make any concessions at all. It should just hang in there, hopefully without further U.S. censure, stick to the status quo and be ready for what happens.

If the Palestinians resort to a new, all-out Intifada, bombing Israeli cities at will, they should be expelled, period.

How would rapprochement between the U.S. and Iran affect Israel? Would it embolden the Hamas movement in Lebanon and Gaza? In fairness, the U.S. should tacitly give Israel a free hand in taking any preemptive action against any hostile nation threatening to attack.

It might also be a good idea to answer Muslim demands with its own impossible-to-meet counter-demands. Any show of giving in to Muslim pressure should be banned, as the enemy would interpret that as weakness.

Israel is already very good at the fine art of stalling, but it should go beyond that. It should become a little wilier. It might ask for a five mile patrolling zone all around Gaza, confiscating any ship or vehicle carrying war material.

Also, Israel should announce that if it is ever nuked, it reserves the right to attack in double measure any Muslim target in return. If the Wailing Wall or any other Israeli holy place is destroyed, it would have the right to do the same thing in return, including Mecca and Medina.

In short, Israel should tell the world that if the Muslims show no respect for the Jews, they must pay for it. All of these things could of course be couched in the finest of diplomatic language.

Don't give an inch of ground, oh Israel,
It is the ancient highway to defeat and hell.

6. THE COMING OIL CATASTROPHE

Unavoidable due to U.S. laxity

Either the U.S. becomes really serious about the looming energy crisis or it perishes. Due to the recent increase in oil demand by giants such as India and China and of course the U.S. with its growing needs, Western economies are all feeling the pinch. The foreseeable blow may hit like a hurricane.

The snail's pace with which the government, automakers, scientists and other industrial leaders are moving towards alternative energy may very well topple America's position as the world's super-inventive industrial nation. Since the last oil crisis in 1973, the U.S. has just been marking time, waiting for the next crisis to happen.

It is not just its wasteful use of energy or its inefficient and self-destructing urban sprawl with its bizarre traffic snarls on never wide enough highways that are guzzling it up by the mega-barrel, nor even the competition with India and China that is hurting America.

The greatest energy spook that will haunt the generations of the next fifty years is WORLD INDUSTRIALIZATION LINKED WITH OVERPOPULATION. This two-headed monster may eat up the last green wildernesses of the world, as it is already busy at in the Amazon, Borneo and the tropical jungles of Africa and Indonesia.

American business leaders believe the entire world will in the foreseeable future reach the level of western prosperity through better housing, schools and hospitals, with new advances in technology, improved agriculture and food processing, plus an American-modeled grid of paved streets and highways in all the third world countries, together with the whole gamut of supra- and infrastructure servicing ever larger urban conglomerates spreading like inkblots across the globe, followed by rain forests being cut down for new agricultural expansion, deserts irrigated by desalinated ocean-water etcetera. What impact will all this have on planet Earth and its wild inhabitants and on ecology, global warming and the atmosphere? What would this bode for the long-term quality of life?

Realizing that even today the balance between energy supply and demand is precarious, how will this end up a hundred years from now, when the whole world is "developed" and, moreover, world population has risen from 6 billion in the year 2000 to a projected 14 billion in 2100?

Will any U.S. university make a study of the double effect a possible 14 billion world population plus total world industrialization; will have on global warming, pollution, natural resources, wildlife habitat, oceans and fish?

Will the media investigate a possible behind the scenes Arab power play regarding the oil shortages?

Some of us will remember when people on the island of Borneo were burning down their forests at such a rate that the sun dimmed over large parts of Asia for months? How the jungles in the Amazon were indiscriminately cut down, destroying some of the world's most important wetlands?

Now imagine this kind of thing happening all over the world through universal industrialization. The last 50 years has seen a growing American apprehension regarding its diminishing forests, wilderness and rare animal and plant species.

Why not also work for the protection of primitive African and Asian tribes? Why force Western civilization on them? Why must everybody on this earth learn to speak English and spit on the richness of his own language and culture?

Look at what America is doing to its own indigenous people by allowing them to build all those culture-destroying casinos for the benefit of their own money-grubbing lower instincts and the inane public devotion to the god of gambling? What does this do to the Indian children, their language, lifestyle, diet, dignity and history?

Not long ago I attended a University lecture at which a professor, helped by graphs and statistics, "proved" that the world could easily provide work, food, and shelter for 24 billion people by the year 2100. I asked him what kind of lifestyle one would enjoy by then, considering our present inability to control pollution, congestion, city crime and so on. He had no direct answer. Maybe those things could not be factored into his graphs.

Think of the immense, almost incalculable energy demand and consumption in a fully industrialized world. Are oil, coal and water inexhaustible? Viewed in the long term, total world industrialization based on the Western habit of depleting the earth's energy resources should urgently be reevaluated.

When will the Americans themselves become the world's leaders in making the crucial switch to new sources of energy? This issue is so critical that an EMERGENCY should have been declared long ago, the same as when 9/11 happened.

The energy crisis and the war on terrorism are clearly intertwined in the Middle East, but the U.S. is so hampered by its short-term views and decisions that it can only think of more laws like the Homeland Security and Patriot Acts to underline its paranoid reactions to Chicken Little. I hear it almost every day now: "America is not getting it".

It is to be hoped that the 2009 administration will consist of two parties that will make the solution of the double-edged dilemma of war and energy their first and foremost priority.

Bankrupting the Muslim oil world

If the U.S. cannot be the first in the development of a brand-new energy technology, it might as well kiss its previous record of being number one in new inventions good- bye.

But I have been told that the internal U.S. oil industry is not all that enthused about new energy and hybrid cars. The U.S. has oil in the ground too, but when it was $ 40 a barrel, it hardly paid to operate the oil wells. When prices were in the neighborhood of $120, the home oil industry made a bundle. It was floating on the high world market.

In other words, the idea of boring for more oil in off-limits polar areas does not come from a government that is worried about the oil shortage and high gas prices, but from a group of people that want to develop new oil fields to cash in on the shortage and would not mind seeing the shortage last.

Yet almost every school child knows by now that the high prices the U.S. pays for Middle East oil indirectly finance the war on terrorism. The Saudi Arabians use the money to help the Palestinians in their intifada against Israel. Even bin Laden's father in Saudi Arabia, who ran a business building roads for the government, rode on the tail end of the oil income. And the bin Laden clan, as a result, is filthy rich, thanks to America.

Carmen bin Ladin, sister-in-law of Osama, who wrote "Inside the Kingdom", tells us about the bin Laden brothers, all multi-millionaires and members of the bin Laden Organization, who worked for the Saudi princes.

Sometimes a half million dollars lay openly on a bench or a chest in the living room.

Wherever a new mosque is to be built or Islam promoted, whether in Europe or the U.S., the Saudi family finances it. As to bin Laden, his chief hobby became financing terrorism.

In his fatwa, he scolds the U.S. for "stealing" the oil riches from Islamic soil, yet he knows full well that his own riches indirectly come from the country he is fighting. It is plain deceit, but the answer to this conundrum is actually quite simple if you know a little about Muslim logic: he is simply following Mohammed's dictum "War is deceit".

Summarizing, both the U.S. globalization policy and the continuation of its present oil policy are going to hurt the U.S. in the long run and can be defined as faulty, short-term vision. The American population is starting to realize that its oil-driven prosperity machine is vulnerable. Even India and China will feel the boomerang effect of its oil-based industrial expansion race.

To solve its energy crisis—and do so ahead of the rest of the world—the U.S. should enact immediate emergency legislation regarding alternative energy. Prizes should be awarded for the best research and practical application resulting therefrom. Funding should be provided for industry, universities and individuals competing for solutions. The media should get behind it, publishing and supporting progress.

I do not believe that American oilmen would have to be afraid of losing their shirt through new energy inventions. There will always be need for oil, but if the new technologies could lead to a reduction in the U.S. import of oil so that the price of gas and diesel would stay in the neighborhood of say $2.50 a gallon, everybody could live.

If it should ever come to the point where an invention should lead to the complete replacement of oil, the government should agree to buy the oil wells on U.S. soil, so the owners can invest in the new technology enterprises.

Can atomic energy be used for the mass-production of hydrogen compressed in cylinders for use in cars and trucks instead of gas tanks?

Let us now proceed to the ultimate oil strategy that could defeat all Muslim insurgency forever and how suicidal it is for the U.S. to remain lax in the face of the looming oil catastrophe.

Part of the strategy is the idea that U.S. oil dependency, if cut in half for example, could once again lead to energy self-sufficiency and thus strengthen and renew the economy.

But that is not the number one advantage. First and foremost it means that the U.S. would kill the fundamentalist cash cow. It would be analogous to Reagan's trick to break the Russian war machine and economy with his Star Wars project.

Destroying the Muslim capacity to finance its march to world domination from the petrodollar would lead to the breakdown of all Muslim power in the world. IT WOULD BANKRUPT ISLAM. It would impoverish bin Laden! There would be no more need to fight world terrorism on the present scale. No more U.S. soldiers dying in ambushes. The U.S. could freely impose its demand that Muslims abjure the jihad verses and might even be able to educate the Arabs abroad. What is more, World War III could be avoided.

The U.S. is in peril. Now is the time to take drastic action to terminate its oil dependency and prevent the coming disaster. Suppose the Arabs responded by turning the oil taps on again? The biggest mistake the U.S. government could then make would be to stop the rush for new energy;

the Arabs could play that game forever and win. Will the U.S. fall for it, like in the 1970s?

Believing that the Arabs would act in the interest of the U.S. is like the Allies believing Hitler in 1938 at Munich.

Bankrupting Islam is the key to a responsible U.S. exercise of its great power in suppressing Muslim tyranny and terror. **The President, under whose administration the Muslim oil world is destroyed, would become the greatest U.S. president ever.**

7. TRIMMING THE ISLAMISTS' BEARDS

Which way are they going?

But you may ask: what will happen to all those Arabs who will suffer if the national oil income is slashed in half when America invents new oil technology? We must not forget that almost none of that income ever reaches the masses—it goes to the extended clans of the ruling class in support of their luxurious lifestyle (think of Saddam Hussein and the Saudi royal family with their chains of palaces), while a large part goes to the acquisition of weapons. The poor will always remain poor.

On the other hand, the sheikhs are likely to sell off some or all of their foreign investments to replace the lost oil income.

It cannot be denied that the Muslim economies would shrink and that this in turn could result in hardship among the lower classes. Large Middle East regions would revert to their former agricultural, caravan-driven craftsman economies; in other words, to a simpler structure of self-sufficiency. And of course they would stay polygamist, breeding by the millions every year.

As a side result of the above factors there could be an increase in the migration of jobless to Europe and North America, especially to Canada which needs more people to develop the country.

An unpleasant side effect of this exodus is the poor integration of Muslim believers into a secular society. The unavoidable presence of the clerics amongst them translates into mosque sermons in which the faithful are warned to stay aloof of the "decadent" unbelievers as much as possible except for work, resulting in ghettoization.

Perversely, the clerics then blame their isolation on the host country, causing unrest, vandalism (Paris!), a welfare mentality and, sometimes, the demand for sharia law in the ghetto. That these sociological phenomena are more prevalent in Europe than in North America is partly due to the European disdain for guest labor and a government hands-off policy, whereas in North America instead of ghettos we see a more dispersed type of Muslim neighborhoods (Detroit) in a society that is individualistic and in constant flux.

The one aspect that is the same on both sides of the ocean is the mosques popping up wherever a sufficient amount of believers live. The clerics who teach the whole Quran are obliged to stress the future duty of jihad and the (supposed) inferiority of Western beliefs and morals.

The real difficulties begin when a burgeoning Muslim community in any given area demands the privilege to wear Islamic apparel when driving or in school, or to stop work for their prayer rituals, and is then met by the 'unforgivable sin of "resistance to Islam" as Western rules forbid it.

These problems have become acute in France, which has the largest Muslim population in Europe—ten percent. When Muslims reach 30% of the population, they are advised by the clerics to demand national legislation protecting and promoting Sharia law.

This has already happened in Kosovo, once a Serbian Orthodox bulwark. And it is in the works in the Sudan, Kashmir and other places.

With a massive influx of jobless poor from all over the Middle East, Muslim percentages in some areas of Europe could reach 30% in 25 years, pushing its eventual Islamization into fairly clear focus. This brings us back to the already mentioned paradox that the Muslims win even when they lose.

What would happen if boatloads of jobless Arabs anchored off the American shores and slowly starving to death, were refused entry? Would American hospitality and humanitarianism win over caution and give them "refugee" status like we grudgingly do to Cubans and other Latinos?

Could that, with the help of the clerics, lead to the Balkanization and Islamization of America?

Can illegal immigration be stopped?

The U.S. is already in quite a mess over the illegals from south of its border, building fences and walls at an enormous expense to keep them out. Is this necessity or insanity?

It is an undeniable fact that these people do menial jobs at low wages, thus filling a gap in the labor force, providing fruit growers, contractors and farmers with hard to get help, We cannot deny that these "guest workers" help the American economy in a big way.

Therefore, let us make a short diversion to review an easy and efficient method to punish the illegals, satisfy the employers' need for scarce labor, help the government control the situation without spending ridiculous amounts of money and REGISTER the 12 million illegal Latinos in America—all without disrupting the economy:

1) Order all employers to identify and register all illegal at a local office, with penalty warning;

2) Deduct $ 1.00 an hour from each worker towards a national fund to defray expenses for health, education and other costs, so that no worker is a financial burden to the United States;

3) Allow the illegals to remain for the season on the condition that they sign an exit form with a warning of heavy penalties for not leaving the country;
4) No promise of citizenship;
5) Subject must leave with wife, if married, and children, even those born in the U.S.
6) Employer will not be fined or harassed if complying;
7) Issue of an alien card to the holder as a "guest worker";
8) Procedure to be repeated if subject crosses the U.S. border the next year without getting caught;
9) No further construction of border fences or walls.

This procedure would ensure that all 12 million illegal Latino immigrants would eventually be registered, possibly at the rate of one million a year. It would be preferable to a measure that would allow eventual citizenship, because that would open the floodgates to another 12 million illegals.

It should also be applied to illegal Cuban, African and Asian illegal immigrants.

The ground rule would be to allow them to work but make them pay for it. Everybody would win: the employer, the worker, the government, the economy and the security of the country.

Keep only the good Muslims

Realistically, the only effective way to sift the loyal Muslim immigrants from the bad ones is to demand that each be asked to forswear and abjure all jihadic texts in the Quran and not teach or promulgate them, on penalty of deportation. Those that refuse to do so are by definition anti-American and illegal.

But I predict the U.S. government will not dare to openly confront Islam, even though such a measure is ten times as efficient in controlling subversive Muslims as the dragnet of the Homeland Security and Patriot Acts.

The U.S. is too submissive to Islam, but ironically submission, according to the Quran, is the first step towards Islamization.

We politely cater to some Muslim wishes and they respond by calling us (as "unbelievers") the vilest of animals (Sura 8:55). Why don't we have the nerve to tell them: "Listen, the West has made it to the top in technology, housing, health and education thanks to hundreds of years of hard work, but you want to drag us back down to the Middle Ages? You believe we are evil, but we believe you are evil".

Thus each side would know exactly where it stands. If the Muslims want to leave instead of abjuring jihad, so be it. Better now than 25 years from now. At this stage and knowing about Islam what we know now, cowardly appeasement is only delaying the inevitable—continuous Muslim hate, infiltration and insurgency against the West until they win.

The way the U.S. is going about finding terrorist cells in the homeland through a costly, police-inspired, vaguely targeted apparatus of indiscriminate legislation, is the way Stalin tried to eliminate opposition by suspecting practically everybody. It is the sure way towards totalitarianism.

The only target should be the Muslim insurgency. The 9/11 crisis was not the result of white or black insurgency.

What must be controlled is the Muslim insurgency and the only effective way to do that is by separating the good Muslims from the bad ones through clear, targeted legislation that can be applied without violence and without restricting the freedom of the rest of the public at airports, borders or on the streets.

You may object: "But the vast majority of Muslims have shown that they are peaceful and non-insurgent". Let us not be naïve. There are three kinds of Muslims in America: first, the insurgent cells or jihadists, or whatever you want to call them, secondly those that give shelter and food and thirdly those that contribute to the cause through their regular contributions to Muslim "charity" and the coffers in the mosque. That takes care of all of them. What ties them all together is the belief that Islam is the only true religion and that each must make his or her contribution towards the eventual victory of Islam.

The government assumes that there are still Islamic jihad terrorist cells in America, but that, since 9/11, they have gone underground. They may rent space in warehouses of wealthy Muslim entrepreneurs or in a complex that includes a mosque and a school, or they may meet in ordinary-looking houses. And some of these locations may also contain caches of weapons, anti-American educational literature or computers with coded data.

The cardinal fact about Islam we must never forget is that it is not just a religion or that most Muslims in the U.S. look peaceful, but that Islam itself is militancy for Allah. No Muslim believer, regardless of his or her peaceful behavior, can be loyal to the U.S. and at the same time to a religion that has as its primary goal the overthrow of all governments run by "unbelievers". A Muslim's oath of allegiance is therefore deceit.

This duplicity is not noticeable now, because Muslims are still a small minority and the clerics teach them "patience" as required by the Quran. In the long run the clerics will call the peaceful Muslims to Jihad against the unbelieving Americans and if they do not obey they will be threatened with eternal hell fire.

The U.S. should not consider the short-term peaceful Muslim attitude as the norm for all time, but as the long-term prospect of Jihad that will be forced on every Muslim believer.

When the call from the clerics comes, whether it is 50 or 75 years from now, they MUST take up arms to deal with any American who "resists" peaceful submission to Islam. America will become like Kosovo, Lebanon and the Sudan, racked by never-ending, internal jihad warfare, with Muslims from all over the world streaming in to assist.

The U.S. bringing in thousands of Iraqis who have helped in the war is therefore sheer insanity. The clerics will still teach them the whole Quran. They will still be told that ultimately Americans must submit to Islam, if need be by 'holy war".

There is no better time than now to protect the freedom of future Americans through measures undoing and preventing the apparent perjury committed by Muslims when they take the oath of allegiance. If they remain true to the whole Quran with the violent jihadist texts, their oath is not worth the paper it is written on. Lest we forget, Mohammed approved of deceit.

I can already see and hear the protests by many legislators claiming that forced disavowal of certain Quranic texts would be religious discrimination. Well, if that is so, then the U.S. should not jail any Muslim insurgents either, because they act purely in obedience to their religion. The

U.S. does not get it. In Islam, religion, politics and deceit are not separate. They are one.

That objection set aside, the U.S. government should take the all-important step of deporting all clerics who refuse to abjure the violent jihad verses. That might cause fundamentalist objections, but the U.S. might also attract intellectuals from the Middle East who advocate toning down the violent side of Islam. Serious dialogue for a more peaceful interpretation of the Quran could thus start in America.

Also, a "Muslim reform movement" might find a positive echo in the Middle East, as more Muslims conclude that a toned down Quran might be not be such a bad idea after all.

Will American denial prevail?

Iraq, the oil crisis, World War III and Muslim world domination are all part of a chain binding us to a future that will be disastrous if we allow it to shackle us. .

We can break out of the shackles if we turn the tide on Al-Qaida through the creation of a strong Shia bloc and the development of new energy replacing oil.

If the U.S. would regard more oil drilling as only a short term band-aid and start concentrating immediately on new energy sources, it would be a sure step towards keeping its top economic and military position in the world.

It would free its hands in the Middle East and be strong enough to withstand any new large-scale military threat from any direction, preventing a new World War. If not, it will decline or go under.

Unfortunately, the U.S. looks at everything in the short term. If something is not an urgent problem at the present, it will wait and dicker as with the ghost of a Hitler in 1939 until it's too late, possibly losing millions of its soldiers in a Third World War. Seeing no immediate signs of great danger, it will take no long-term measures to protect its people.

The grand plan for repair that should have been adopted   remains only a sketch gathering dust in the attic. The house of America will weaken in the winds of change, until it is splintered by the coming hurricane of millions of Asian and African Muslim filling the vast hollowness of America's short-term political construct like the waves that swept the depths of New Orleans.

8.   THE ARMENIAN GENOCIDE

Debate and denial

The 1915-1916 massacre of Armenian Christians is almost a blueprint of the methodical mass murder through which, in an incredibly short time, the Muslims enlarged their territory in the 600s and 700s. All "unbelievers" who fought their advance or merely defended themselves were mercilessly cut down by the Muslim militants and the women and children enslaved—an entire nation thus Islamized in one generation.

We noted this "efficiency" in Mohammed's savage extermination of the Banu Quraiza tribe in 627 A.D., one of the first jihads. All subsequent elimination of "resisters to Islam" throughout the centuries was the mirror image of that early example set by Mohammed.

The bloodbaths in Turkish Armenia followed exactly the same pattern. Every protest, every plea by the Armenians for moderation was considered "resistance to Islam" by the Turks in terms of the jihad verses (listed in chapter 4). Either the Armenians submitted or were killed.

In a hundred years Americans may very well find themselves in the same position.

Years earlier, under the Ottoman rulers, several groups of Armenians were murdered, each time in larger numbers and always on the grounds of resistance or the mere suspicion or rumor thereof.

We will review them to gain an insight into the Muslim minds of those days, as they were set afire by the jihad spirit. It will happen to us in the future if we do not prepare a plan to stop the Muslim colossus.

This is now a critical issue in view of recent attempts to throw a more temperate light on the bloodied scene, acquitting the Turkish government of some of its culpability and ascribing the deaths of the hundreds of thousands of Armenians during the forced marches to the "unforeseen and unplanned" effects of mass starvation over which the government had no "control".

One of these revisionists, Guenter Lewy, wrote an extensive article in the December 2005 issue of "Commentary", in which he redefines the 1915-1916 Armenian deaths in Turkey as a "disputed genocide". This type of historical reconstruction is generally referred to as revisionism, a genre that is quite popular with certain critics.

Evidently there are also other motives for rewriting history. Turkey, which has applied to join the European Union, is adamant that the whole Armenian thing be forgotten as though it never existed and some Europeans have embraced that idea to a certain extent. Others want Turkey to show rational and factual grounds for its claim of non-culpability. The result is a stalemate.

The central issue, according to Lewy, is the extent to which the Turkish government premeditated the deaths. His conclusion is that this cannot be proven because of a lack of reliable documentary evidence. Secondly, he points out that the Armenians brought the catastrophe on themselves by siding with the Allies when war broke out in 1914. In effect, he argues, the Armenians committed treason by working for the defeat of their own country. By and large, this is the Turkish line too.

However, there is evidence that disproves the above allegations. Firstly, the Turks declared war on the Armenians (jihad} before the death marches. Secondly, the existence of mass graves is known, though denied by the Turks who will not allow access. Thirdly there is documentary evidence.

Morally viewed, there is a striking resemblance between the horrible aspects of the Armenian deportation and the deliberate starvation of the Ukrainians under Stalin in 1932-1933 that caused the deaths of over 8 million people. It was Stalin's response to the Ukrainian farmers' refusal to give up ownership of their valuable lands and property. His regime then hit the farmers with such excessive crop levies that they were not only deprived of seed grain for the next crop, but did not even have any of their own grain to eat. They just starved to death.

The Ukrainian farmers' opposition to collectivization had made them "enemies of the state" and the state retaliated with deadly terror. Tens of thousands of farmers and their families were thus forced to leave for lack of food and died on the roads of hunger, disease, cold and exhaustion in unspeakable misery.

Reduced to walking and crouching skeletons, they were very much like the later Second World War victims of the hideous Nazi concentration camps, targets of the ugliest state terrorism possible.

What is terrorism?

Many historians have struggled with a clear definition of the word terrorism. Actually, there is little or no difference between state and insurgent terrorism, not just because of the slaughter and brutalizing of women and children, but because insurgent terrorists aim to become the state and once in power, enforce their will through state terrorism.

You may remember that the French Revolution was largely the work of terrorist rebels, who after gaining power became known as the "Reign of Terror", slaughtering so many members of the aristocracy that in the end all resistance by the elite was smashed. The Nazi Blackshirts (e.g. Kristallnacht) and the Bolshevik communists (killing the Mensheviks) both started out as terrorists. After gaining power, they continued their terror by jailing and murdering the opposition. Terrorists, therefore, are groups of evil people with evil goals, guided or deluded by evil, anti-social ideologies.

The specific twist in Muslim terrorism is that it is done in the name of a religion that promotes violence against any other religions as a virtue. In an unguarded moment President Bush once called it an evil religion—shortly after 9/11 if my memory serves me correctly—but never again. Since that "slip" he regularly used the term "evil ideology", but even that had to be replaced by a "softer" description.

The Islamic clerics oppose modern education in secular subjects (including science), decry human rights and consider women inferior to men—all of which has resulted in poverty, ignorance and prejudice.

In Muslim thinking, we get our freedom of thought and speech through Satan. What we call freedom is "licence and disobedience" in Muslim terms. To us a peace treaty is the end of war, whereas Muslims consider it a pause for regrouping.

To us, a deal is a deal, to a Muslim a deal means the deception of the infidel. When Arafat was raked over the coals by President Bush after breaking his promise not to import more weapons, he just continued his enigmatic Cheshire cat grin. He knew that "war is deceit".

Muslim terrorism has a lot in common with Naziism and Communism. It is totalitarian, forbids a free press, bans books, tolerates no opposition, is undemocratic, opposes basic human rights and believes it must be triumphant in the entire world.

After Naziism and Communism, Islam, as a terrorist organism, is the new international threat to world freedom.

In his "The Burning Tigris - The Armenian Genocide and America's Response", Peter Balakian convincingly shows

114

that the economic disparity between the poor, clerically-educated Turks and the better-off, well-trained, industrious Armenians had been a constant source of jealousy and friction for many generations.

Defined as second-class citizens (dhimmis), the more prosperous Christians were often vilified to the authorities as being proud and looking down on their Muslim neighbors. As a result, the Armenians were often forced by the local tribal leaders to pay extra local taxes on top of the dhimmi levies.

If and when the extra burdens became so exorbitant that the Christians were forced to complain, the more radical Muslim elements of the village were allowed by the clerics to take "loot" from the "resisting" infidels in any way they could.

Eventually, conditions for the Christians became so critical that desperate groups of farmers went to the central government for protection. However, the local leaders always succeeded in distorting the Christians' grievances to such an extent that the government sent soldiers to restore order, ensuring several of the Christian appellants were killed.

Similar unbearable conditions prevailed in the Ottoman-held Balkans where in 1876 a massive Christian tax uprising in Bulgaria led to a Turkish reprisal in which fifteen thousand men, women and children were massacred.

The Quran calls Christians vile animals and even today Muslims refer to Jews and Christians as monkeys, dogs and swine, with the implied notion that they can be treated as such. Chapters 5 and 8 of the Quran contain many exhortations by the Prophet to use terror against "resisting" unbelievers.

Even peaceful protest against barbarity, corruption and the stealing of Christian boys was considered resistance to Islam.

The upshot of the Bulgarian massacre was the 1877-1878 Russian-Turkish war, in which Turkey was defeated and forced to grant independence to large parts of the Balkan, including Serbia.

But all was for naught. Britain and France, wary of increasing Russian influence in the Balkans, heeded untrue accusations by the Sultan during the peace negotiations and connived to have most of the Russian conquests returned. The Sultan for his part blithely ignored his own obligations in the terms of the treaty and kept harassing the "infidels" as if nothing had ever happened. Islamic war is deceit.

Exactly the same thing had occurred after the previous Russo-Turk conflict of 1853-1856, the notorious Crimean War. Roman Catholic France and Protestant England teamed up with Turkey against Russia, each for its own political agenda to defeat Russia, thereby propping up a corrupt Muslim regime that would do nothing but bleed, plunder and desecrate a group of fellow-Catholics.

The European powers still had not learned the lesson from the fall of Constantinople {Byzantium} in 1453 in which Catholic Europe refused to help its Greek Orthodox brethren in Christ against the Muslim.

Had the city been rescued, keeping the Byzantine Empire in a position of strength as a buffer against further Muslim inroads, the benefits to Roman Catholic Europe would have been immense and far-reaching. For one thing, the rift between the two main religious faiths might have healed over time. Secondly, Muslim power in the Mediterranean area would have been greatly reduced, diminishing the threat to Europe.

But feelings between the Holy Roman See and the Byzantine Patriarch had been strained ever since the 1054

Great Schism between the two great movements. During the Fourth Crusade in 1204, "schismatic" Byzantium was conquered by France and Venice, two Catholic powers, who sacked the city in a horrible bloodbath. The city's defense works were severely damaged at that time and once again when the Greeks briefly retook it from Rome.

The catastrophic fall to the Muslims of the great center of Catholic civilization in 1354 was due both to its weakened defenses and the refusal of the two religious rivals to stand together against the common enemy.

Its once great glory—the Christian provinces of Syria, Palestine, Egypt and parts of North Africa—were lost and gone forever. Europe lay open to the onslaughts of the islamizing armies using their well-honed terror tactics.

Mark this; the mistakes of the past can haunt a civilization for hundreds or even thousands of years. Will America heed the warning signs?

Due to its geographic location between the Mediterranean and Black Seas, the ancient homeland of the Armenians was often fought over by Russians and Persians, later to be conquered for good by the Turks.

Russia, because of its religious affinity and also for strategic reasons, was a natural defender of the oppressed Armenians in Turkey. In spite of the duress of communist dictatorship, the people of what had become Soviet Armenia eventually fared better than their Turkish brethren.

In the eleventh century the Armenians, fleeing from the Seljuk Turks, found a haven in Cilicia in the southeastern part of the peninsula, which became known as Little Armenia. During the Second Crusade in 1204 the Russians protected them there.

When Cilicia was lost in 1375, a little over twenty years after the fall of Byzantium, the hapless Armenians had to accept their former minority role as despised dhimmis in

Muslim Turkey all over again. They endured it for hundreds of years

Armenian treason?

Between 1850 and 1870, the Armenian church officials protested time and again against the unfair daily Muslim extortion, discrimination, humiliation and hostility by the Turks. So it was only natural to look to their Russian friends for protection. Whenever the Russians pushed into Turkey, they were welcomed as liberators.

Had the Sultans had more sense, they would have protected this prosperous, income-bringing part of the country for their own interest, stopping all further invasions by Russian armies trying to protect the Armenians.

The argument of Armenian treason is therefore not well taken. Protests against unfair taxation and civil disobedience are not the same thing as treason. They happen all the time. By sucking the Armenians totally dry, the religiously one-eyed Turks wilfully threw the desperate Armenians into the arms of the Russians.

Like the Ukrainians later, the Armenians were trying to bring a grossly inhuman tyrant to reason. They had a right to look elsewhere if their own government did nothing to protect its own citizens and treated them as enemies.

Over two hundred and thirty-five years ago the American colonies, protesting unfair taxation, fought the mother country and were also accused of treason. However, the word "treason" should never be applied to people rebelling against tyranny.

Besides Cilician Armenia, other Armenian provinces like Erzerum, Bitlis, Diarbekur, Van and Sivas made up the original Armenian heartland—part of the former Anatolia. They had their own cherished Armenian language.

The Armenians were an honest, God-fearing people that, through hard work, had become prosperous and numerous, earning them the envy and hatred of the backward Muslim majority; the government marked them as a political threat because of their friendship with the Russian Orthodox people.

The 1894 and 1895 indiscriminate massacres by the Turkish government were a prelude to the 1915-1916 slaughter, a link in the chain of violence and murder that, from the 1870s on, had came to be meted out against the Armenians as punishment for rebelling against the most ruthless, systematic government exploitation of their honest daily labor.

There is an uncanny, eerie resemblance to the Biblical account of the prosperous Jews in Egypt who in the eyes of the Pharaoh had become such a multitude that they presented a socio-political danger to the country.

One can also see the thread of cruel retribution against any kind of opposition to Islam running through the massacres, in literal obedience to the Quanic verses prescribing hardness and mortal violence against those of the unbelievers that do not submit to the Islamic yoke as a dhimmi or slave without any rights.

No doubt the same methods were used in the early Muslim conquests of the Orthodox lands of the former Byzantine Empire. Only the literal application of the Quranic commands in those bygone days can explain why so few Orthodox Christians survived in Syria, Palestine, Egypt, Eritrea and other Asian and North African areas. Ethiopia and Lebanon were the last two countries with a majority of Christians until recently. They are now threatened by Islamic violence and decimation.

Therefore, extermination as the primary motive must be reckoned with in the Turkish massacres of 1915-1916, an aspect that has not found mention in Lewy's review.

The 1915-1916 deportation deaths cannot be separated from previous Muslim attempts at decimation of the Christian enemy. In the following pages we will follow the historical trail from 1894-1895 through 1909 to 1915-1916.

Consistent religion-inspired murder

By 1892 the Armenian people of Sasun in Bitlis province had been campaigning for fair taxation and protection from the rapacious Kurds for several years. The Sasun group, headed by the Henchak party, an organization of impoverished Armenian farmers, petitioned the government for relief from the Kurdish tax agents who made it impossible for them to make a living anymore.

The next year, the Kurds turned the story around, falsely telling the central government that Sasun was in open rebellion, a crime that, according to the Quran, is punishable by death. Consequently, the year 1894 saw an orgy of retaliatory burning, looting and killing. Thousands of men were murdered, women and girls raped, pregnant mothers disemboweled, babies hacked to pieces and young boys taken captive (stolen) to be re-educated in Islam and trained as soldiers to eventually kill their own people. (Reports of identical Muslim behavior in the Sudan have reached the West in recent years—though much "deplored", except for some hand-wringing, no action was taken.)

When news of the 1894 massacre reached Europe, there was universal revulsion and outrage, but it only led to the official formulation of a proposed code of human civil rights as a model for all nations.

Encouraged by the international furor of wrist-slapping, naïve Armenians from several areas got together and presented a petition for reform to the sultan's residence in the capital on October 1, 1895.

Again, this action was duly interpreted by the clerics as "resistance to Islam" by unbelievers, punishable by death Sura 5:33 says; "the punishment for those who fight against Islam and His Apostle AND STRIVE TO MAKE TROUBLE IN OUR LAND is this: they shall be murdered or hanged….." etcetera.

Since the words in the Quran are supposed to be the last Revelation given to mankind, they supersede anything ever said by Moses, the prophets, Jesus or others, counting as much today as they did nearly 1400 years ago

Hence it is easy to discern the religion-inspired terror and fanaticism in what is happening today in Iraq, Afghanistan, Sudan, Nigeria, Chechnya and elsewhere, even in the 9/11 attack. All the ambushes, kidnappings, beheadings, and road bombings are designed to drive the unbelievers out of Muslim lands, because they "oppose Islam".

It cannot be repeated enough that when a Muslim fights unbelievers, even the most heinous bestiality is done for the glory of Allah. As a result he does not feel the slightest pang of guilt. This psychological trait was also present in the thoroughly brainwashed S. S. men who became so devoid of normal human feelings of sympathy that they could butcher Jewish men, women and children without any remorse or scruple.

After the "S. S." Turks and Kurds had gorged themselves on the Armenian loot and blood, a bit of a lull ensued, allowing American relief workers, supported wholly by private donations, to reach the hardest hit Armenian provinces in 1895-1896.

But the U.S. government had refused to intervene politically while Armenia burned and bled—exactly like Europe.

Abdul Hamid II, the Sultan of the Ottoman Empire since 1876, was highly suspicious of the "Americanization" of Christian Armenia by the relief effort that introduced American methods to revive the devastated agricultural areas. He relished the still passionate public and clerical resentment against the Armenians, itching to re-ignite the holy war against the Christians, through which his troops would deal them a final, mortal blow.

Meanwhile, the relief groups precariously waded through the still smoldering villages and remaining hostilities, providing emergency medical supplies to the roofless, weakened survivors and assisting with the repair and replacement of broken-down agricultural equipment.

The fields around many devastated villages were reseeded in the summer of 1895. The workers had to be careful, as the destructive Muslim terror machine kept moving farther east towards the Persian (now Iranian) border to "complete" their task of punishment.

They heard the fearful survivors' tales of Muslims taunting wounded and dying Armenians with the words *"Where is your Christ now?"* as they went on killing and robbing the defenseless people. The horror stories kept coming in right up to 1897.

After the widespread destruction ended, health conditions among the survivors worsened. Whole districts were hit by typhus, adding daily to the already staggering death toll.

Though almost all Armenians were unarmed by order of the government, there were a few pockets of resistance. Groups only numbering in the hundreds, with old muskets and sabers, clubs and even pitchforks, were able to put up a heroic defense, inflicting heavy casualties on thousands-strong Muslim regiments, only to be tricked into promises of safe passage and massacred in cold blood after disarming– Muslim war is deceit.

Though the atrocities became widely known in America and were roundly condemned by the Press, the U.S. Congress passed only a weak resolution against the Turkish government.

The latter then allowed the American Red Cross, under the capable leadership of Clara Barton, entry into the country in January 1896. She and her people worked tirelessly amongst the Armenian wounded, bringing in food and equipment to relieve the terrible suffering.

But the killings could not be undone—the storm of terror had left the entire Armenian sector of Turkey in ruins and ashes, while the carnage still continued in isolated areas that could not be reached by the Red Cross in time.

In order to once and for all draw major attention to the still ongoing looting, burning and bloodletting, a small band of desperate young Armenian Dashnak party members decided on a unique publicity stunt—the take-over (not robbery) of the Ottoman Bank of Constantinople.

The hoped-for publicity was achieved. The entire European press supported the Armenians, pushing their governments to intervene militarily. Notwithstanding the extremely critical situation, the European powers could only muster a series of harsh condemnations and veiled threats in case the enormities did not stop.

The Sultan, not seeing any serious preparations for armed intervention, took his cue—Europe was weak and Allah is strong. Buoyed by the clerics, he ordered a massive "revenge action" against the Christians. The troops were called out and, in a frenzied orgy, killed and looted thousands more Armenian families, both in Constantinople where the rebellion had taken place and in the city of Egin where the rebel leader lived.

The European press again blasted their governments for their lax stand, leading only to more "dialogue" and infighting.

While the U.S. government held to its official policy of non-interference, it did send several ship loads of food, equipment and medicine. Its response to the catastrophe is strangely similar to its present attitude regarding the killings and displacement of non-Muslims in Darfur as sanctioned by the Sudanese Sunni government. Harsh words—little action.

Had the Russians crossed the border or even supplied sufficient arms to the young Armenian men, the situation might have been reversed and ended up with a small autonomous Armenian region, but its hands were apparently tied as well.

Thanks to the inaction of the European powers and the U.S., thousands of Christian villages were wiped off the face of the earth and hundreds of churches and schools burned to the ground.

The devastation in the Kurdish areas was even greater. People, packed in sanctuaries, hoping they would be safe, were lured out on promises of exile, only to be cut down as soon as they came out. Priests were decapitated, Christian books and Bibles torn to pierces, even the corpses were desecrated and looted. The cries of "Alluha Akbar" (Allah is great) accompanied the vilest murders. Rapes and abductions were rampant.

A couple of European warships in the harbor stood idly by with no orders to interrupt the daily, deathly rampages.

In some villages, churches filled with fleeing Armenians were put to the torch, burning all those inside alive. Elsewhere, church members were put to the choice of either converting to Islam on the spot or being killed en masse. In some cases, people gave in and hundreds were forcibly converted. The Quranic texts regarding those who give in (desist) and those who resist were followed to the letter.

See Sura 2: 192, 193; Sura 8: 39, 61; Sura 9: 14, 29, which give instructions regarding those who desist or convert.

The mass killings of 1894 to 1896 throughout Turkey, including Constantinople, ended the lives of some 250,000 Armenian men, women and children—sacrificed, one might say, on the altar of political expediency, namely the containment of Russian power. A "strong" Turkey against the "Russian threat" was considered more important than a quarter million Armenian Orthodox Christians.

The Young Turks against the Christians

Eventually, in 1908, the corrupt rule of the half-mad old Sultan was overthrown by a new generation of "Young Turks" who were tired of a tyranny that affected and degraded the whole population. Slogans of "Justice for all" were heard all over the country.

The Armenians in Cilicia naively thought it applied to them as well and became so enthused (and fooled) by the new prospect of equal rights that they started celebrating in the streets of Adana, the capital, expecting independence for the province. Immediately, the all-seeing clerics insinuated to the Young Turks that the Cilician Christians were a threat to the new government and Islam. The result was an unsurpassed bloodbath in Adana the next year, 1909.

The British Vice-Consul, Doughty Wylie, who lived not far away, rushed to the city and was the only person who, with a group of loaned Turkish soldiers, was able to stop some of the killing, looting, and burning. But he could not be everywhere and by the time the rampage subsided through sheer glut of loot, some two thousand Armenians lay dead. Even the Turkish police shot several Armenian seen trying frantically to save neighbors, women and children.

The hope of a Christian Cilicia was buried with the dead.

The World War I deportation horrors

The 1915 massive deportation of the Armenians from Turkey is a constant in the long series of attacks we have followed on previous pages. It is obvious that it would not have been due to unforeseen difficulties encountered during poorly organized long-distance transportation.

To begin with, there is evidence that the Germans with whom the Turks were allied, had infused the Turks with their theory of racial purity, convincing them that the elimination of the Greeks in western Turkey and the Armenians in the east would be the sure way to Turkish unity and greatness.

The clerics supported the idea for their own pan-Islamic goals and so, on May 27, 1915, the Deportation Law against the Armenians was adopted, ostensibly because the latter favored the Allied cause and were considered enemies of the state.

But something more ominous had preceded this law. In November 1914 Holy War had secretly been declared by the clerics against the Armenians as "resisting unbelievers". This was literally a death sentence and no amount of "unforeseen travel difficulties" rhymes with that.

Holy war meant that all Christian male deportees were fair game to be slaughtered anywhere, anytime after that date. The women could be raped or made concubines and the young boys taken for future army duty and re-education as Muslims. The edict was amplified by opening the jails and promising the criminals forgiveness and Paradise for killing Christians or having them converted to Islam.

It is impossible to describe the horror that followed in the form of hunger, dirt, disease, despair, looting and killing by the Kurds and criminals looking for loot and Paradise.

As the deportation march slowly wended its way eastward, the overnight bivouacs at the designated stopping places became nightmares of rape, looting and killing by the lawless bands of Kurds and criminals.

Somehow, after unbearable torture, the looters found out that a woman hid some gold in her baby's rectum A frenzied search began and as many of the little ones as could be found were butchered and their insides 'checked". Whole piles of baby bodies were found later, unburied, decaying off the road.

Heaps of skeletons along the hundreds of miles of desert road to Syria increased as the weeks dragged on. Emaciated, wounded or sick, without water, the stragglers sat by the roadside and died or were killed. Only a fraction survived and reached Syria, where many more succumbed through lack of food, shelter and purposeful neglect. An estimated total of one and a half million Armenians perished.

Mr. Lewy mentions that not all deportees were forced to march on foot—many were able to buy train tickets. But from the evidence of eyewitnesses and survivors it has been shown that only fifteen percent of the train travelers were still alive on reaching their destination in Aleppo, Syria. The rest died during the stopovers.

At every one of those camping spots, the infidels were robbed of money and valuables. The scenes of torture, degradation and death were almost unparalleled in recorded human history and in the memory of people then living.

The more battles the Turks lost in the war against the Allies, the more the tempo of killing increased. Self-defense in the city of Van was equated with treason since Turkey was at war and punished accordingly—250 of the city's Armenian elite were arrested and murdered. Other areas with the slightest connection to Van were treated in the same way. The bereaved women were generally allotted to Muslim men, their children taken from them and "re-educated" in Muslim families.

Monstrous things happened to young Christian women. Some were raped bent over and then forced to squat on small wooden crosses in the ground, sharpened at the top, causing horrible wounds and the most hellish degradation and pain ever suffered by human beings. As they lay screaming, their captors taunted them with shouts of "Where is your Jesus now?"

Regular wooden crosses were also used. An eyewitness saw sixteen Armenian girls hanging, nailed hands and feet, in Malatia near the Euphrates River.

An Armenian survivor of one of those bestialities told of how a group of Muslim horsemen at a place in Diyarbekir province played a game whereby she and other young girls, one sitting in front of each rider, were thrown upright onto long swords planted in the sand where they would be impaled. In a miss, the girl was scooped up again for another "try". The best "hitter" got a prize. Those poor girls died for us as martyrs to show just what may await us if we keep appeasing religious fanatics and being careful not to hurt their tender feelings.

Should we not honestly tell the Muslims that we are just as tired of their inhuman religious outrages as they are of our so-called secular democratic decadence? Why do we take all their insults and not tell them that their morals stink?

Whereas Muslims think that Western decadence is part and parcel of the Christian heritage, it actually comes from people stepping outside of it.

Muslims also believe that Jesus will come back soon to inaugurate his perfect Kingdom—as a Muslim.

Summarizing the 1915-1916 Armenian genocide

- The so-called temporary Law of Deportation, enacted May 27, 1915, by the Turkish government regarding the Christian Armenians was preceded on November 14, 1914 by an edict of Jihad or Holy War against all Christians in Turkey, issued by the Sunni Sheikh-al-Islam, Mustafa Bey.

- This gave permission of looting and killing Armenian Christians to all male adult Muslims in Turkey, including the "chetes" (released convicts), who were TRAINED to harass and kill the deportees from the time they were driven out of their homes to arrival in Syria.

- All the measures against Christians were carefully prepared by the Committee of Union and Progress (C. U. P.) of the Turkish government, with the specific goal of ensuring the largest amount of deaths possible, both during the forced foot marches and the cattle train transports.

- The Armenians were lured into the death marches and trains on false promises of safe conduct.

129

- The killings, mistreatment, abductions, looting, burning and forced conversions followed a strict pattern of Jihad warfare against infidels as laid down in the Quran and as exemplified by the Prophet.

- The 1915-1916 massacres were identical to the methods used in the killings of Christians in the 1870s and 1890s.

- Turkey still owes the Armenians hugely for Genocide, both in reparations and a corridor to the Black Sea.

- At the November 1922 Lausanne Conference the three conquering nations, England, France and Italy, with approval of the U.S., sacrificed Turkish Armenia on the altar of lucrative new trade and OIL. All four owe the Armenians.

9. WORLD ISLAMIZATION

The figures speak for themselves

There is absolutely no doubt that, comparing the present demographic changes and developments with the past and projecting them into the future, the Islamic population of the world will some day outnumber the adherents of any other religion, including the non-religious. When will this happen and what will be its consequences for the West? How will the world look in a hundred years?

World population grew from roughly one and a half billion in 1900 to six billion in the year 2000 a quadruple increase. At that rate of growth, there would be 24 billion people on earth by 2100.

But the available statistics predict a slower rate, which can be shown by the following table:

1900	–	1.5 billion
1930	–	2 "
1975	–	4 "
2000	–	6 "
2025	–	8 "
2050	–	10 "
2075	–	12 "
2100	–	14 "

These figures are slightly higher than those in the late editions of "Time Almanac" and "World Almanac and Book of Facts", which show a 2050 projection of around 9.5 billion.

Has the Muslim part been underrated? After careful study my calculations indicate that a 2 billion world population increase every 25 years is more correct. I will show evidence and consequences.

Population projections Muslim countries—thousands

Country	2000	2025	Increase	%	Religion %
Afghanistan	25,889	48,045	22,156	85.5	84 Su, 15 Sh
Albania	3,490	4,306	0 816	28.5	70 M, 30 Chr
Algeria	31,194	47,676	16,482	53	Su
Azerbaijan	7,748	9,429	1,681	21	90 M, 5 Chr
Bangladesh	129,194	179,129	49,935	39	88 M, 11 H
Burk. Faso	11,946	21,360	9,414	79	50 M, 40 P
Chad	8,425	14,360	5,935	70	50 M, 50 Chr/P
Comoros	578	1,160	582	101	86 M, 14 Chr.
Cote d'Ivore	15,981	27,840	11,850	74	60 M, 37 P/Chr
Djibouti	451	841	390	86.5	94 M, 6 Chr
Egypt	68,360	97,431	29,071	42.5	94 M, 5 Chr
Eritrea	4,136	8,438	4,302	104	50 M, 50 Chr
Ethiopia	64,117	98,763	34,646	54	50 M, 40 Chr.
Gambia	1,367	2,678	1,311	96	90 M, 9.Chr
Ghana	19,534	28,191	8,657	44	30 M, 62 P/Chr
Guinea	7,466	13,135	5,669	76	85 M, 8 Chr
Indonesia	224,784	287,985	63,201	28	87 M, 6 Chr
Iran	65,620	91,889	26,269	40	89 Sh, 10 Su
Iraq	22,676	44,146	21,470	95	65 Sh, 35 Su
Jordan	4,999	8,223	3,224	64.5	96 Su, 4 Chr
Kazakstan	16,733	18,565	1,832	11	47 M, 44 Chr
Kuwait	1,974	3,559	1,585	80	85 M
Kyrgyzstan	4,685	6,066	1,381	29.5	75 Su, 20 Chr
Lebanon	3,578	4,831	1,253	35	70 M, 30 Chr
Libya	5,115	8,297	3,182	62	97 Su
Forward	**750,040**	**1,076,343**	**326,303**		

Country	2000	2025	Increase	%	Religion %
Malaysia	21,793	34,248	12,455	57	68 M
Maldives	301	623	322	107	97 Su
Mali	10,686	22,647	11,961	112	90 M
Mauritania	2,668	5,446	2,778	104	100M
Morocco	30,122	43,228	13,106	43.5	99 Su
Niger	10,076	20,424	10,348	102.5	80 M
Nigeria	123,338	203,423	80,085	65	50 M, 40 Chr
Oman	2,533	5,307	2,774	109.5	100 M
Pakistan	141,554	211,675	70,121	49.5	77 Su, 20 Sh
Qatar	744	1,208	464	62	95 M
Saudi Arabia	22,024	50,374	28,350	128,5	100 M
Senegal	9,987	22,456	12,469	125	92 M, 8 P/Chr
Sierra Leone	5,233	11,010	5,777	110	60 M, 40 P/Chr
Somalia	7,253	15,192	7,939	109.5	99 Su
Sudan	35,080	64,757	29,677	84.5	70 Su, 20 Chr
Syria	16,306	31,684	15,378	94	74 Su, 10 Chr
Tajikistan	6,441	9,634	3,193	49,5	80 Su
Tunisia	9,593	12,760	3,167	33	98 M
Turkey	65,667	89,736	24,069	37	95 M, 5 Chr
Turkmenista	4,518	6,514	1,996	44	89 M, 9 Chr
Un.Arab E	2,369	3,444	1,075	45	96 M
Uzbekistan	24,756	34,348	9,592	39	88 Su, 9 Chr
Yemen	17,479	40,439	22,960	131	99 M
Forwarded	**750,040**	**1,076,343**	**326,303**		
TOTAL	**1,320,561**	**2,016,920**	**696,359**	**53%**	**(average)**

Total number of Muslim countries listed: 48

Abbreviations: M = Muslim; Su = Sunni; Sh = Shia;
                        Chr = Christian; H = Hindu; P = Indigenous

Source: World Almanac and Book of Facts, 2001.

One of the striking aspects of the above table is the tremendous contrast in population growth between the several Muslim countries. Seeing that Muslims multiply at a much higher rate than the rest of the world, could these differences hide discrepancies due to poor statistics keeping and enumeration methods?

Saudi Arabia's natural annual increase is listed in the 2001 World Almanac and Book of Facts as 3.145 %, which translates into more than doubling its population in 25 years, possibly quite accurate. An increase of close to 3% per year leads to an almost exact doubling in 25 years, Examples: Comoros (3.046%), Gambia (2.95%); Iraq (2.88%), Niger {2.83 - 3.1%),

The different rates of growth in Iran and Iraq give pause to think. Also, the low increases in Algeria, Bangladesh, Ghana, Indonesia, as well as those in Kazakstan, Kyrgyzstan, and Uzbekistan seem open to question.

Deducting the non-Muslim minorities in the Muslim countries and adding the Muslim minorities in others, such as in Russia, the rest of Europe and China, added only about 60 million to the total of 1,320,000,000 which raised the total Muslim world population in my figures to 1,380,000,000 in 2000, as compared with the 1,155,000,000 cited in the 2001 World Almanac (p. 692).

The chart can also be used for pinpointing Muslim trouble spots, indicated by the Muslim percentages in the right column. Where "infidels" are a minority, they have to live under constant threats of discrimination and Islamization, while being in the majority may mean underground insurgency.

The following chart will show the amazing rate at which the Muslim world population grew from the 1950s to 2000, based on existing statistics. They show a fearsome, steady annual expansion rate of 2.3% that can be readily projected into 2025.

Muslim population expansion at 2.3% annually
Amounts in millions 1950 – 2000 and projected to 2025

1950	400						
1951	419	1961	526	1971	661	1981	830
1952	429	1962	538	1972	676	1982	849
1953	439	1963	551	1973	692	1983	868
1954	449	1964	564	1974	707	1984	888
1955	459	1965	577	1975	724	1985	909
1956	470	1966	590	1976	740	1986	929
1957	481	1967	603	1977	757	1987	951
1958	492	1968	617	1978	775	1988	973
1959	504	1969	631	1979	793	1989	995
1960	515	1970	646	1980	811	1990	1018
1991	1041	2001	1307	2011	1641	2021	2060
1992	1065	2002	1337	2012	1679	2022	2107
1993	1090	2003	1368	2013	1717	2023	2156
1994	1115	2004	1400	2014	1757	2024	2205
1995	1140	2005	1432	2015	1797	2025	2256
1996	1167	2006	1465	2016	1838		
1997	1194	2007	1498	2017	1881		
1998	1221	2008	1533	2018	1924		
1999	1249	2009	1568	2019	1968		
2000	1278	2010	1694	2020	2014		

The 2.3% annual increase is much higher than shown in the Almanac, but as can be seen, very consistent. It equals 75% for a 25-year period. The Almanac figures showed an increase of 53% each 25 years. This difference can be solved by averaging.

When working on the Almanac figures, I discovered that its Muslim population projections for 2025 are sharply lower than its own increase percentages suggest. To take a few examples, the countries of Chad, Nigeria and Pakistan are shown as having a natural increase rate, respectively, of 3.31%, 2.644% and 2.937%, all close to the doubling factor of 3% we noted. However, the end projections for each of these three countries are way below doubling. In other words, the statisticians expect the population increases to slow down a bit in the near future

But it is by no means proven that the Muslim birth rates are going to level off over the next 25 years. The Muslims have kept the same habits for over centuries and it is doubtful they will change much in the near future.

The 53% rate increase for a 25-year period that the Almanac figure led to, must be considered too low. I think the 1950 – 2025 increases shown on the previous page are in line with a much more realistic, consistent trend spanning three quarters of a century. But I will use averaging as a reasonable compromise – the medium between the Almanac's data of 53% and my high of 75% on the previous page, namely a 64% increase every 25 years, as worked out in the following diagram.

Year	Projected world population	Muslim growth at 64% per 25 years	Growth left for Non-Muslim world
2000	6 billion	1.3 billion	4.7 billion
2025	8 billion	2.1 billion	5.9 billion
2050	10 billion	3.44 billion	6.56 billion
2075	12 billion	5.5 billion	6.5 billion
2100	14 billion	9 billion	5 billion
2125	16 billion	14.75 billion	1.25 billion

The West's doom is in sight

The astounding fact that emerges from the above table is that by the year 2100 Muslim population expansion will have overwhelmed the rest of the world by a margin of 9 to 5.

The reader can clearly see that stagnating Western population growth and strong Muslim expansion will inevitably lead to "absorbing" Western culture starting from

2050 on. At that date the chart shows a decline in Western growth from 6.56 to 6.5 billion and so on, until in 2125 there are only 1.5 billion Westerners left. How is that possible?

This is because by the time world population has reached 16 billion, Islam's growth will have reached 14.75 billion, which leaves only 1.25 billion Westerners, due to absorption by Islam, either THROUGH FORCED CONVERSION OR ELIMINATION.

The old, proven method of killing the husband, appropriating the wife and re-educating the children will likely be used wherever the Muslim clerics decide it's needed.

There cannot be a shadow of a doubt but that this is what the Prophet had in mind when he talked about killing the infidels until there is no more opposition and the religion is only for Allah—global Islamic domination.

There could already be big trouble by the year 2025, when the Muslim numbers will have reached one third of the world's non-Muslim population (2 billion versus 6 billion, see previous page). We all know that Western population growth lags way behind Islamic expansion, but some may not realize how critical the situation is already becoming.

As far back as 1982, the World Almanac and Book of Facts (page 352, footnote 6) reported that the Islamic Center in Washington DC had counted 1 billion Muslims worldwide.

In 2008, a quarter century later, the same Center upped that figure to 2 billion, way above my conservative estimates. But will the above facts spur the U.S. and Europe into action?

If the U.S. sticks to its methods of dealing with each problem on an ad hoc basis, micro-managing like a city council, whether in Iraq, Afghanistan or elsewhere in the Middle East, it will lose its grandeur. It must look into the future, far into the future, to 2050, 2075 and 2100. The struggle against international terrorism calls for a totally different global strategy, one that will save Western civilization from extinction.

Can the U.S. forgive Russia for its slow pace towards democracy and stand shoulder to shoulder with it in the fight against looming Islamic world domination?

When will there be a bonus for students learning Arabic so they can read Muslim newspapers and understand Arabic TV? The government is short thousands of dual language speakers in all sectors.

Why does the U.S. government wait for another oil crisis to happen? Is it worth continuing an oil dependency that will enslave the U.S. until it lies shackled on the ground, begging the Arabs for a little more of the scarce stuff? Can U.S. oilmen be convinced they will be doomed anyway, unless they too change direction and start investing in new energy systems? That they owe this to their children and grandchildren as well?

When will the government support and give incentives to universities, research institutes and business in the field of new energy? Why is America not the first to invent brand new systems? If another country makes a breakthrough first, it will become number one in the field and the U.S. will be number two. Will this become a trend?

Will the media join the fight for the future of young America as well as for continuing freedom from tyranny?

Does the government have enough insight into the future and the courage of statesmanship to change direction in the Middle East through a pact with the Shias, winning the war against the real enemies, Saddam's Sunnis, without losing any more soldiers? Do they know they have it in their combined, powerful hands to cause a sea change in the

Middle East, forever pitting a strong Shia bloc against the Sunni majority, to the advantage of the U.S. and the rest of the Western world?

Does the U.S. know it can bankrupt the Muslim economy by inventing new energy systems? That in doing so, it has the key to eliminating the funds that finance terrorism? That this is a peaceful method of destroying the power of Islam? That it could prevent a third World War?

Only when America forces the Muslims totally on their knees will they finally see that Allah is not all-powerful. And they should be told right in their faces. Maybe some will come to the conclusion that their religion should be reformed.

It is critical that Democrats and Republicans lay aside their different agendas concerning international politics and reach common ground vis-a-vis the almost irreversible threat of Muslim world domination.

If they cannot accomplish that, they can look forward to only one party: the Party of Allah.

POSTSCRIPT

Beginning in 2001 shortly after September 11, on reading Peter Bergen's warnings, I started investigating the hard to untangle Islamist insurgency problem. The 9/11 event left the entire Western Hemisphere alarmed and exasperated, forcing many researchers to try and find the motives for it as well as its long range future implications and remedies.

I was not at all familiar with the background of the unprecedented growth of Islam, little realizing that it was the product of centuries of religious conquest and forced conversion, based on the forever binding instructions of the Prophet Mohammed. All I had learned consisted of basic historical and geographical data, never the inherent religious factor behind it nor the immoral methods used.

For example, I knew that the English, Dutch and French colonizers bought black slaves from African dealers for their oversees possessions, but not that these middlemen were Muslims who wiped out whole villages of "infidel" blacks, then sold them as cattle.

Not until I discovered that a religious movement such as Islamism can never be permanently defeated by conventional warfare; secondly, that the West's huge oil dependency plays a large role in its own weakness in the Middle East and thirdly, that the relentless impetus of an ongoing Islamic population explosion will in the near future lead to the displacement and destruction of our Western culture did I begin to realize the magnitude of the trap the free world is in.

BIBLIOGRAPHY

MUST READ

Balakian, Peter. *The Burning of the Tigris – The Armenian Genocide and America's Response.* New York, 2003.

Bergen, Peter J. *Holy War, Inc. – Inside the Secret World of Osama bin Laden.* New York, 2001.

Bin Ladin, Carmen. *Inside the Kingdom – My Life in Saudi Arabia.* New York, 2004.

Darwish, Nonie. *Cruel and Usual Punishment – The terrifying global implications of Islamic Law.* Nashville, Tennessee, 2008.

Hiro, Dilip. *The Essential Middle East – A Comprehensive Guide.* New York, 2003.

Ibn Warraq. *Why I am Not a Muslim.* Amherst, NY, 1995.

Maren, Michael. *The Road to Hell – The Ravaging Effects of Foreign Aid and International Charity.* New York, 1997.

Swarup, Ram. *Understanding the Hadith – The Sacred Traditions of Islam.* Amherst, NY, 2002.

Other important sources on Islam, Middle East, and Terrorism

Armstrong, Karen. *Islam – A Short History.* New York, 2000.

Armstrong, Karen, Geraldine Brooks, Thomas Cleary, Bernard Lewis, V.S. Naipaul, Huston Smith, William T. Vollmann, Fareed Zakaria e.a. *Inside Islam – The Faith, the People, and the Conflicts of the World's Fastest Growing Religion.* New York, 2002.

Bawer, Bruce. *While Europe Slept – How Radical Islam is destroying the West from Within.* New York, 2006.

Beamer, Lisa, with Ken Abraham. *Let's Roll.* Colorado Springs, 2002.

Bello, Walden. *Dilemmas of Domination – The Unmaking of the American Empire.* New York, 2005.

Benjamin, Daniel, and Steven Simon. *The Age of Sacred Terror.* New York, 2002.

Bennett, William J. *The Death of Outrage – Bill Clinton and the Assault on American Ideals.* New York, 1998.

Buchanan, Patrick J. *The Death of the West – How Dying Populations and Immigrant Invasions Imperil our Country and Civilization.* New York, 2002.

Campbell, John C. *Defense of the Middle East – Problems of American Policy.* New York, 1960.

Carew, Tom. *Jihad! – The Secret War in Afghanistan.* Edinburgh, Great Britain, 2000.

Carter, Jimmy. *The Blood of Abraham – Insights into the Middle East.* Boston, 1985.

Clarke, Richard A. *Against All Enemies – Inside America's War on Terror.* New York, 2004.

Curry, Dayna, and Heather Mercy. *Prisoners of Hope – The Story of our Captivity and Freedom in Afghanistan.* New York, 2002.

Dershowitz, Alan W. *Why Terrorism Works – understanding the threat, responding to the challenge.* New Haven, 2002.

Finucane, Ronald C. *Soldiers of the Faith – Crusaders and Moslems at War.* London, Great Britain, 1983.

Frantz, Douglas, and Catherine Collins. *Death on the Black Sea – The Untold Story of the STRUMA and World War II's Holocaust at Sea.* New York, 2003.

Gabrieli, Francesco, transl. E.J.Costello. *Arab Historians of the Crusades.* New York, 1969.

Glenny, Misha, revised and updated. *The Fall of Yugoslavia – The Third Balkan War.* New York, 1993.

Hoffman, George W. *The Balkans in Transition.* Princeton, 1963.

Huntington, Samuel P. *The Clash of Civilizations – Remaking of World Order.* New York, 1997.

Ibn Warraq, editor. *The Origins of the Koran – Classic Essays on Islam's Holy Book.* Amherst, NY, 1998.

Jacobson, David, with Gerald Astor. *Hostage – My Nightmare in Beirut.* New York, 1991.

Laqueur, Walter. *No End to War – Terrorism in the Twenty-First Century.* New York, 2003.

Lewis, Bernard. *What Went Wrong – Western Impact and Middle Eastern Response.* New York, 2002.

Lewis, Bernard. *The Crisis of Islam – Holy War and Unholy Terror.* New York, 2003.

Lippman, Thomas W. *Understanding Islam – An Introduction to the Muslim World.* New York, 1995.

Machiavelli, Niccolo; transl. George Bull. *The Prince.* New York, 1981.

McCauley, Martin. *Afghanistan and Central Asia – A Modern History.* Harlow, Great Britain, 2002.

Murphy, Carlyle. *Passion for Islam – Shaping the Middle East: The Egyptian Experience.* New York, 2002.

Olson, Barbara. *The Final Days – The Last, Desperate Abuses of Power by the Clinton White House.* Washington, DC, 2001. (posthumously)

Parfrey, Adam, ed. *Extreme Islam – Anti-American Propaganda of Muslim Fundamentalism.* Los Angeles, 2001

Petterson, Donald. *Inside Sudan – Political Islam, Conflict and Catastrophe.* Boulder, CO, 1999.

Posner, Gerald. *Why America Slept – The Failure to Prevent 9/11.* New York, 2003.

Powers, Thomas. *Intelligence Wars – American Secret History from Hitler to Al-Qaida.* New York, 2002.

Quran, The. Any Translation.

Randal, Jonathan C. *Going All The Way – Christian Warlords, Israeli Adventurers, and the War in Lebanon.* New York, 1984.

Rashid, Ahmed. Jihad – *The Rise of Militant Islam in Central Asia.* New Haven, 2002.

Sada, Georges, – with Jim Nelson Black. *Saddam's Secrets – How an Iraqi General Defied and Survived Saddam Hussein.* Brentwood, TN, 2006.

Seale, Patrick. *Abu Nidal – A Gun for Hire. The Secret Life of the World's Most Notorious Arab Terrorist.* New York, 1992.

U.S. News and World Report, Staff. *Triumph Without Victory – The Unreported History of the Persian Gulf War.* New York, 1991. (477 pp.)

Yant, Martin. *Desert Mirage – The True Story of the Gulf War.* Buffalo, NY, 1991.

Jewish Sources

Haddad, Heskel M., M.D., as told to Phyllis I. Rosenteur. *Flight From Babylon. Iraq, Iran, Israel, America.* New York, 1986.

Johnson, Paul. *A History of the Jews.* New York, 1987.

Karetzky, Stephen, and Peter E. Goldman, editors. *The Media's War against Israel.* New York, 1986. (423 pp.)

Laqueur, Walter. *A History of Zionism.* New York, 1976.

Laqueur, Walter, and Barry Rubin, editors. *The Israel-Arab Reader – A Documentary history of the Middle East Conflict.* New York, 1984. (704 pp.)

Marcus, Jacob R. *The Jew in the Medieval World – A Source Book: 315-1791.* New York, 1969.

Margolis, Max L., and Alexander Marx. *A History of the Jewish People.* Philadelphia, 1934.

Meir-Levy, David. *Big Lies – Demolishing the Myths of the Propaganda War against Israel.* Los Angeles, 2005. (per my visit to Temple Judea, F.M., 2-20-2007)

Potok, Chaim. Wanderings – *Chaim Potok's History of the Jews.* New York, 1984.

Rabin, Leah. *Rabin – Our Life, His Legacy.* New York, 1997.

Siilverberg, Robert. *If I Forget Thee, O Jerusalem – The dramatic story of how American Jews and the United States helped create Israel.* New York, 1970.

Thomas, Gordon, and Max Morgan Witts. *Voyage of the Damned.* New York, 1974

Periodicals

An-Naim, Abdullah Ahmed. *The Islamic Counter-Reformation.* In New Perspectives Quarterly, winter 2000, pp. 29-36.

Hollak, Rosan, and Laura Starink De Staat, de Jihad en de Islam (panel). *In NRC Handelsblad,* Nov. 3, 2001, pp. 8-25, Netherlands.

Hurgronje Snouck, C. La legende qoranique d'Abraham et la politique religieuse du prophete Mohammed. In "Revue Africaine", Vol. 95, 1951, pp. 273-288, France.

Kurtlantzick, Joshua. *China's Global Reach.* In "U.S. News and World Report", August 6, 2007, pp. 38-45.

Lewy, Guenter. *The First Genocide of the 20th century?* In "Commentary", December 6, 2005, pp. 47-52.

Mayer, Hans Eberhard. *Literaturbericht ueber die Geschichte der Kreuzzuege.* In "Historische Zeitschrift", 1969, pp. 641-736, Hannover, Germany.

Morse, Edward l., and James Richard. *The Battle for Energy Dominance. In "Foreign Affairs"*, March-April 2001, pp. 16-31.

Pinault, David. *Teaching about the Jesus of Islam.* In "America", Nov. 28, 2005, pp. 14-16.

Robinson, Simon, James Nachtwey and Samantha Power. *The Tragedy of Sudan.* In "Time', October 4, 2004, pp. 44-63.

Spencer, Williams. *The Middle East.* In "Global Studies" (Annual), 212 pages. Dushkin Publishing, Guilford CT, 1986.

Tallwar, Puneet. *Islam in the Balance.* In "Foreign Affairs, July-August 2001, pp. 58-71.

Weaver, Kenneth F. *Our Energy Predicament.* In "National Geographic Special Report on Energy", February 1981, pp. 4-23.

INDEX